HUSBANDS FROM HELL

By
JAN KING

Illustrated by
BOB McMAHON

CCC PUBLICATIONS • LOS ANGELES

Published by

CCC Publications
20211 Prairie Street, Suite F
Chatsworth, CA 91311

Copyright © 1991 Jan King

Manufactured in the United States of America

Cover design © 1991 CCC Publications

Illustrations © 1991 Jan King & CCC Publications

Cover & interior art by Bob McMahon

Cover production by The Creative Place

ISBN: 0-918259-32-0

If your local U.S. bookstore is out of stock, copies of this book may be obtained by mailing check or money order for $5.95 per book (plus $2.00 to cover sales tax, postage and handling) to: CCC Publications; 20211 Prairie Street, Suite F; Chatsworth, CA 91311.

Pre-publication Edition — 5/91

First Printing — 7/91

Second Printing — 9/91

To my darling Mark; in whom I've placed my trust,
my friendship, and all the love that's in me.

ACKNOWLEDGEMENTS

I would like to give thanks to a very special person, my sister Karen Bracy for contributing a good deal of the material set forth in "Husbands." So all you gals will want to shake her hand and all you guys will want to just shake her until her brains rattle. And in the spirit of sisterly love, I can say in all honesty, anything offensive in the book was solely her idea.

Also special thanks to her Husband from Heaven, Al Bracy, for coming up with the title of the book. My love to you both for your constant support and unparalleled childcare contribution while I was out promoting my books. And my love and thanks to my two boys, Michael and Philip, for their support and understanding during the time I had to be away from them for promotional work — even though they kept handing me more airline tickets immediately upon my return.

To my publisher, Mark Chutick, who asked not to be mentioned, I would be remiss if I did not express my gratitude for his continued belief in me and my abilities as a writer. He has my everlasting admiration for his genius in producing and promoting my books. Thanks so much, Mark — and now you can move the gun away from my temple.

And last but not least, I want to thank my editor Cliff Carle for another expert job. I always learn so much from Cliff when we edit a book, but this time I was happy he learned something from me: he learned he would be wise to remain single for life.

J.K.

CONTENTS

INTRODUCTION

Men. We love them, we marry them, and now we have to put up with them. So, whether you're a newlywed or an old vet with several marriages under your belt, sit back, relax, and get in the spirit of "Husbands From Hell" by having a few belts while you read it.

The current psychobabble, used to excuse men who are totally infuriating, is to say, "Nobody's perfect." *Perfect?* Who are we kidding? Most women will settle for *highly irregular* at best. So read on while "Husbands" strips open and lays bare the truth about the most irritating aspects of every type of husband on the planet — without apology. You're also going to get some tips about how to best cope with the various aggravating behaviors of husbands plus some advice on how to fulfill their own peculiar sexual needs. And I do mean PECULIAR in most cases.

And we all know how men have great senses of humor about themselves, so I have counted on them to take this book in the spirit of fun in which it was written and have a good laugh at their own expense. In fact, I was so sure they would, that after months of writing in a bulletproof vest and dodging golf clubs on a trajectory aimed at my word processor, "Husbands From Hell" was completed with only a few minor injuries to the author.

Women love to get together in a variety of public places and swap intimate and inappropriate tales about their husbands. And the men should be glad we do. It saves them approximately $6 or $7 billion collective dollars a year in psychiatric fees to have us intellectually and calmly analyze our respective marital situations with each other rather than with a trained money-sucking professional. This way when our guys screw up, they won't have to pay for it twice — at home *and* at the shrink's office, too.

These impartial female discussions have been recognized and approved by most male psychologists as a valid course of therapy and are identified by their technical name: "bitch sessions." Some doctors use the term to describe the oral activity itself, and others use it to label the women engaged in the conversations. It all depends upon the doctor's individual perspective *and* how many ex-wives he is supporting. In any case, out of these sessions comes a lot of wisdom, well thought-out advice, and some deeply profound statements such as: "Men. Who the hell needs 'em?"

So I have chronicled their various behaviors and detailed every type of husband and his own peculiar traits in common with every other male of the species. And all this collective information is conveniently categorized for easy reference. Women will be able to recognize the make and model of their husbands in some or possibly all of the chapters. And if your model does happen to appear in ALL of the chapters, it's probably time for a trade-in.

But keep in mind that even though we love our husbands, there's nothing wrong in finding a little humor in the idiosyncrasies we've discovered after years or, in most cases, *days* of marriage. So now it's up to you to open up new lines of communication with your man by reading to him the chapter you feel describes him best. Then enter into a meaningful dialogue with him — armed with a baseball bat and catcher's mask, of course.

CHAPTER 1

HYGIENE HABITS FROM HELL:

The Slob
vs.
The Perfectionist
(Anal Retentive) Husband

3

SECTION A: THE SLOB HUSBAND

JOB DESCRIPTION: PICKUP ARTIST

Almost every woman on the planet enters a marriage taking for granted that her husband's mother painstakingly instructed him in everything he needed to know about personal hygiene, cleanliness and neatness. However, we soon find out this only held true when your man was living with HER. Within milliseconds after saying "I Do," the groom's memory patterns of these habits are wiped out. Automatically, he will discard his tie, cuff links, and garters in his wake as he walks back down the aisle. His memories of order and neatness are so obliterated that the only use he remembers for a hanger is where to park a plane.

Men can not help this behavior. It has been genetically programmed into their chromosomes ever since Adam left a trail of fig leaves behind him in the Garden of Eden for Eve to pick up. Even the snake went around carelessly shedding *his* skin throughout the garden, leaving it for her to clean up, too.

In light of what we now know, I suggest that the marriage vows should be rewritten for future generations to reflect a more realistic picture of what women are really committing their lives to:

"I promise to love, honor, obey, pick up his dirty socks and underwear, and in general, keep his cage clean 'til death or homicide do us part...."

THE LAUNDRY BASKET: A SHOT IN THE DARK

Women have tried for years, unsuccessfully, to train their husbands to put their dirty clothes in the laundry basket after removing them. Now, mind you, these are the *same* guys who have been able to shoot a basketball straight through the hoop in one try since they were five years old. So why is it they can NEVER figure out how to get their clothes into a laundry basket possessing a four foot square rim which is located three inches away from their feet? Do we need to install a hoop over it? Some wives have even gone so far as to hook the basket onto the guy's belt — but even that didn't work. No matter where you place that laundry basket, his dirty clothes will always end up strewn all over the room, and his hamper will remain forever empty. There is just no way possible to teach a man to do this. You will be able to train your thickheaded Schnauzer, the squirrels in your yard, and any female over the age of six weeks to do it. But the bad news about your slob husband's ability to comprehend these tasks comes down to this bottom line — his brain waves are a *flat* line. We're talking irreparable brain damage when it concerns learning how to pick up after himself.

THE SLOB HUSBAND'S BATHROOM HABITS: LETTING IT ALL HANG OUT

Some married couples have been heard to brag, "Our honeymoon lasted for over a year." Dream on! Your honeymoon will be over the minute you begin to share a bathroom with your beloved. This is why many savvy builders are pushing homes with separate "his" and "hers" bathrooms. Costly? Yes, but worth every penny. The marriage will last longer — like about 150 mortgage payments more.

Guaranteed to elicit a range of emotions running the gamut from mild irritation to the desperate last resort of swigging down Drano, here's a list of the **Slob Husband's "Top 10" Most Irritating Bathroom Habits...**

#10 DISCOVERING EMPTY TOILET PAPER ROLL AFTER YOU'VE SAT DOWN

Husbands go through a roll of toilet paper faster than a roll of Bounty paper towels. Maybe this is because they keep the slogan "quicker picker-upper" in mind as they happily wipe away. Whatever the case, the wife can expect to find a perpetually empty toilet paper roll at any given time of the day. Slob husbands do not "do" refills. They would rather suffer the ignominious consequences than have to move their butts off that warmed seat to fetch a refill. So women must never again, for their own safety and peace of mind, sit on the john without a backup roll clasped to their bosom.

#9 DISCARDING HIS DIRTY CLOTHES WHILE SITTING ON THE TOILET

For the life of us, women will never be able to figure out why men feel compelled to remove their dirty Jockey shorts (which smell like the horse left something in there too) and their dirty socks while they're sitting on the toilet seat for an hour reading dirty magazines. Then they leave them in little piles around the "throne." The question we all need answered is, *WHY do they do this?* Does removing one's socks and underwear automatically improve one's reading skills? Or is it just that the reading

7

material is making their socks sizzle?? We are thoroughly confused by this ritual. It is certainly not a common practice for us women to remove our bras and pantyhose in order to read "Cosmo" — unless Helen Gurley Brown instructs us to do so in one of her notorious quizzes.

#8   WAITING FAR TOO LONG TO FLUSH

The slob husband is not the swiftest when it comes to remembering to flush the toilet. He usually waits until he has accumulated a roll and a half of Charmin in the bowl before he decides to pull the chain. Then he leaves the house just as the water in the bowl is cresting over the rim and the contents are flooding out onto the floor, loosening the plaster on your dining room ceiling. This leaves you no option but to go in there armed with hip-wader boots, a Wet-Vac, and a safety net to break your fall when you inevitably come crashing through the rafters.

#7   TOSSING THOSE WET, STINKY, GERMY TOWELS ON YOUR BEDSPREAD

The bathroom of a slob has towel racks which will never see wet towels. He always throws them on the bed after each use. This practice creates an eco-system which supports the growth of great populations of microscopic pond scum on your sheets. It is not uncommon for housewives to begin adding algicide along with the Calgon to the wash. That's so you both won't get out of bed in the morning looking like you were attacked by "The Swamp Thing."

#6 LEAVING THE INDELIBLE BATHTUB RING

The successive soap scum rings your mate leaves around the bathtub year after year can be counted like those of the Giant Sequoia to accurately tell the age of the fixture. (And because he never rinses himself off properly, the ones around *his* trunk can be used to tell his age as well.) In two hours, these rings become harder than cement and would take a team of Merry Maids equipped with a sandblaster to remove them. And even if you can successfully talk the Merry Maids into doing it, it'll cost you big — they charge time and a half for doing bodies.

#5 HIS DRAIN-CLOGGING HAIRBALLS IN THE SHOWER

The burly slob husband with a back like a shag rug will ultimately wreak havoc upon your shower by leaving hair clogs in the drain sizeable enough to trap small rodents. These clogs, made from the kind of curly back hair with the same texture as Brillo, have been known to break the steel blades on a Rotor-Rooter snake. If it only happened, say, every other month, we could handle it. But these guys shed more hair per day than your pet Collie does during the months of summer.

#4 LEAVING SCUZZY, NAUSEATING BEARD SHAVINGS IN YOUR SINK

The slob husband always leaves the beard shavings from his Remington electric shaver and/or nose hair clippings scattered throughout your freshly scrubbed sink. This practice instills a desire to track down Victor "I Liked The Shaver So Much I Bought The Company" Kiam and punch him right

9

in the chops. But exert caution. You may have to follow Victor into his Patriot's locker room and be subjected to sights a lot more graphic than nasal hair.

#3 NEVER AIMING HIS YOU-KNOW-WHAT STRAIGHT

Even though he claims that anatomically he is able to test the depths of the water in the bowl without using his hands, he is still unable to direct his stream with any precision and leaves those tell-tale yellow dribble marks all over the rim, sides, and floor of the toilet bowl. Some women have even reported dribble streams as far away as the sink and shower door. Worse yet, after a night of drinking with the guys, many women find those stains *in* the sink and *on* the shower door.

#2 LEAVING HIS PERSONALIZED AROMATIC SIGNATURE BEHIND

The slob husband is particularly adept at leaving some unbelievable aromas to greet you upon entering the bathroom. These are often the byproduct of last night's time-released burrito.

...And the #1 Top Bathroom Irritating Event...

LEAVING THE TOILET SEAT UP THROUGHOUT ETERNITY

After each successive use, he will always leave the toilet seat upright. When you sit down, depending on your butt size, you will either:

    a. fall in and drown, or

b. freeze your buns off when you make
   contact with the icy ceramic rim

The sobering truth we wives of slob husbands
will have to face the rest of our lives is that we'll
most certainly meet our deaths by being gassed,
drowned, or something worse.

* * *

Many of us will wish that we had married a neat
freak like Felix Unger. But let me caution you that
these types have some pretty extreme bathroom
habits of their own which could ultimately drive you
to do some desperate act like holding your head
under water in their perfectly scrubbed and
sanitized toilet bowl. Let's take a look at this
unusual breed...

11

SECTION B:
THE PERFECTIONIST HUSBAND

THE ANAL RETENTIVE: A MAN
WHO CAN HOLD HIS OWN

Sticking with the subject of bathrooms, the flip side of the coin is the PERFECTIONIST or ANAL RETENTIVE HUSBAND. Let's explore some new Top 10's from the anal retentive's side — and a side, let us add, which doesn't have a particularly pretty view. Although these neurotically neat men may seem at first to be the answer to your prayers, you'll soon be praying that somebody will step in and whisk them off to a halfway house for obsessive-compulsives. Whoever said "Cleanliness is next to Godliness" obviously didn't have an anal retentive spouse. He is one step away from becoming as fanatical as Howard Hughes. The anal retentive will be hellbent on making his environment so sterile that, like the Maytag repairman, the average germ could die of loneliness in your toilet bowl. So at this point, I'd like to present **The "Top 10" Anal Retentive Pain-In-The-Butt-Behaviors...**

#10 EXCESSIVE WIPING

He has installed a dispenser for those pre-moistened rectal wipes which are never disposed of in the bowl after each use, but are fastidiously folded into smaller and smaller squares until they reach the exact proportions of a postage stamp. Then the edges are stapled and the towelette is introduced into a 4" x 6" Baggie, hermetically sealed, and placed with tongs into the bottom of a special wastebasket designated for this purpose. By the way, these procedures are never performed without the use of sterile surgical latex gloves, automatically dispensed from a wall unit each time the toilet seat is lowered.

#9   NUKING TOILET SEAT GERMS

Not only will the toilet seat be found in the "down position" at all times but he will also include:

a. A sanitized paper strip calibrated to the exact epicenter of the seat top, with the edges sealed leaving a 1/8" perfect margin around the rim.

b. An overhead ultra-violet light to fry every last microbe on the seat before the lid automatically comes down and the paper seal is applied.

#8   OBSESSIVE-COMPULSIVE FLUSHING

His Anal Retentiveness never leaves a trail of anything. He is obsessive about flushing between each sphincter contraction, due to his fear of lapsing into unconsciousness from toxic fumes. Once popularly known as the "courtesy flush," he has elevated it into the new art of "flash flushing."

#7   SANITIZING HIS JOCKEY SHORTS

He would never think of leaving his used Jockey shorts by the bowl. Instead, he pre-treats them with Spic & Span, applied painstakingly via a grout brush to remove all tell-tale skid marks, then folds them in quadrants and piles them neatly in stacks of six each at the bottom of the hamper. This is followed by a blast of Lysol spray directed at the crotch, before the hamper lid is closed.

#6   EXCESSIVE WASHCLOTH FETISH

The anal retentive has the sole distinction of always taking a shower *before* he enters the bathtub so he will never leave a dirty ring behind. Always alert not to cross-contaminate from one orifice to the other, he will use separate washcloths labeled "face," "torso," and "nasty genitalia."

#5   COMPULSIVE FEAR OF PUBLIC TOILET SEATS

Obsessive-compulsive cleaning of toilets is not limited to personal bathrooms, either. A-Rs are averse to using any public facility, especially airline bathrooms. More than one anal retentive, in attempting to clean out an airliner's bowl, was inadvertently sucked down the toilet into the tail jet, leaving only his shoes sticking out of the bowl for the next horrified passenger to discover.

#4   UNHEALTHY PREOCCUPATION WITH HIS AIM

Unlike the slob husband who not only misses the bowl, but doesn't come within three feet of it, the anal retentive spends countless hours in the bathroom perfecting his dead-eye aim. He will not only be able to hit the bull's eye on the target he has painted inside the bowl, but can accomplish it even while wearing a blindfold — on his "derringer."

#3 ADOPTING AN ORAL HYGIENE OVERKILL PROGRAM

Anal retentives follow a schedule of conscientiously applied oral hygiene to the point where their gums are so raw from brushing and flossing they'll bleed if they ever laugh too hard. The A-R's lineup of dental hygiene products include such high-tech devices as:

a. the water pik

b. the Interplak with a dozen replacement heads

c. three electric toothbrushes with back up battery packs in case of power failure

d. Plax fluoride: 3 gallon keg on tap

e. specialized tooth scalers manufactured by Ginsu for do-it-yourself plaque removal below the gum level

f. automatic dispenser containing enough unwaxed dental floss to circle the planet three times

#2 INSTITUTING HIS OWN ORAL SEX/ORAL HYGIENE PROGRAM

And because the American Dental Association has not been progressive enough to issue guidelines for a recommended program of dental hygiene after oral sex, he has formulated his own which includes the following products for gargling:

a. Janitor-In-A-Drum laced with yeast killer: 6-gallon dispenser

b. Nair Hair Remover: 32 oz. bottle

...And the #1 Top Anal Retentive Pain In The Butt Behavior goes to...

THE DANGEROUS PRACTICE OF GAS RETENTION

Literally, the anal retentive would rather die than leave a foul smell in his wake (or at his wake, for that matter), so he constricts his anal sphincter and swells up with methane gas. Some have been known to hold gas until they became airborne and floated out the bathroom window. The wife then has to call the Civil Air Patrol and put out an APB on a missing A-R, last seen floating around in restricted airspace somewhere over the residential neighborhood.

* * *

Anal retentive behavior is not just isolated to bathroom habits. It invades every aspect of his, and consequently, *your* life. After being consumed by fanatical attention to meaningless details, you'll come to the realization that this man could definitely benefit from a few near death experiences to put his priorities in order. I have interviewed wives of A-R's all over the country and listened to their horror stories about what they have had to contend with on a daily basis. The result is the following list of some of the quirkier habits and behaviors the A-R breed of husband considers "normal":

1. Alphabetizing soup cans
2. Ironing money and placing it face side up all going the same way
3. Taking an *all-nighter* for an eye test

17

4. Walk-in medicine chests

5. Won't drink milk that has lapsed 1 hour beyond the stamped expiration date on the carton

6. Insists that his boxer shorts be starched and ironed

7. Obsessive sanding and waxing of wooden shoe trees

8. Sneaks into the kitchen at midnight to re-scrub the pots and pans *you* washed after dinner

9. Always uses both electronic and hand signals at all times when driving, leaving other confused motorists in massive pileups

10. Forbids the removal of pillow and mattress tags for fear of breaking the law

So with either choice, these husbands are going to drive you to the same path as certain well-known wives of politicians: drinking large quantities of rubbing alcohol laced with hairspray just to cope with their husband's behavior. Which one would I advise you to pick as your mate for life? Tough call. It's kind of like trying to choose sides between Leona Helmsley and the IRS.

QUIZ I

1. You can identify your slob husband's underwear by:
   a. the rust stains
   b. the way it cracks when he takes it off
   c. his name — written in there since high school gym class
   d. the way they stick to the wall when he takes them off and throws them across the room

   * *all of the above, all of the time*

2. Which item is left in ashtrays by the slob husband?
   a. his navel lint
   b. a wet and slimy chewed cigar butt
   c. cigarette pack cellophane used as dental floss
   d. matchsticks covered with earwax

   * *a,c,d — only on the rare days when he grooms himself*

3. The slob husband insists on saving money by re-using:
   a. condoms
   b. toilet paper
   c. chewing gum
   d. Tucks

   * *a — before the expiration date, however*

4. The slob husband signals he is finished with his dinner by:
   a. wiping his mouth on his tank top
   b. belching, "What's for dessert?"
   c. extinguishing his cigarette in his mashed potatoes
   d. clipping his toenails at the table

   * *too close to call*

5. The anal retentive husband keeps his person scrupulously clean by:
   a. frequent douching
   b. regular flea dips
   c. waxing his "bikini area" weekly
   d. colonic irrigations with Lysol

   * c — *it eliminates the need for b*

6. The anal retentive's childhood is filled with fond memories of:
   a. holding hands with his Mom
   b. holding his pet doggie
   c. holding his breath for 8 hours at a time
   d. holding his bowels for 8 days at a time

   * d — *this would account for his adult personality*

CHAPTER 2

WHITE COLLAR MEETS RING AROUND THE COLLAR:

The Professional
vs.
The Working Stiff Husband From Hell

SECTION A: THE
BLUE COLLAR HUSBAND

For the sake of literally making "broad" definitions, this chapter will be devoted to the discussion of the Blue and White collar husbands. Roughly half the female population will lose their hearts plus some other body parts to guys in the macho hard hat category. These women, desiring a "real man" in their lives, often end up with a lot more than they bargained for. Where and how they found their hunks is a simple matter of knowing the basic haunts of this indigenous species. Besides looking for them at the bottom of the gene pool, they can always be found at the following locations:

1. At any construction site featuring a crane, a caterpillar dirt mover, and steel beams. The guys are easy to spot because they are never actually working. Instead, they're positioned in a line close to the street. This lineup consists of burly construction guys, half of them making smacking and sucking noises. The others are enlisting classic hand gestures while uttering inane phrases to each and every female passing by:

    "Humma humma ... Hey MaMa come ova heah' and show your sweet Papa what you got for him!"

    or

    "Baby, Baby (smack-smack, suck-suck) let me give you what you know you want!!"

Actually, what I would want most at that moment is to bend over and blow lunch all over his hard hat. But hey, I can't speak for everyone. Whatever turns you on.

2. Another place to find your Blue Collar Baby is in the local sports bar. It is frequented by such types enjoying their four-hour lunches (consisting of a dozen brewskis) or their male-bonding Miller Time which goes from after work until dawn. The guys found drinking in here are so tough, the establishment serves Jack Daniels on tap. These burlys prefer munching on a bucket of nails to a bowl of pretzels and swill down mass quantities of beer until they vomit all over themselves. Yes, they really know how to live on the edge.

    But they are dapper guys in their own way. They'll light your cigarette with an acetylene torch. And you can gaze lovingly in their eyes while you take in the aroma of Pennzoil mixed with diesel fuel wafting from their hair.

3. A very unexpected-but-great place to find tough guys is reported to be the laundromat. Even Connie Chung has interviewed some of these single men between spin cycles and ovulation cycles, so it has to be true. Because they don't own a washer and their clothes are filthy most of the time, this is an ideal spot. Even if they aren't wearing their signature blue denim shirts and tight jeans at the time, you can always recognize them. They are the men who don't pull their clothes out of the dryer until they smell something burning. A sure-fire way to introduce yourself is to drop something

lacy, sexy, and preferably D-cupped in front of them. Stand back and watch the mad dash as six of them fight to retrieve it for you. But be cautioned: this garment will have to be run through another wash cycle to remove the inordinate amount of drool stains off it.

4. A sure place that never fails to attract huge masses of Blue Collar men is one of our country's finest sporting events — the Tractor Pull. There seems to be some unknown chemical attraction going on between these guys and large quantities of inflated rubber. Do they get a sexual rush just from hearing those huge tires moan and groan as they strain from the weight of the two bodies rubbing and pulling against each other? Or maybe they just aspire to one day be able to inflate something rubber of their own to those huge proportions? Well, who knows ... anyway this discussion is making us a bit hot under the ole blue collar, ourselves...

Once you have found the macho man of your dreams, here are a few tips about the care and feeding of these guys. DO NOT under any circumstances feed these men "sissy foods" (i.e. quiche, sushi, or anything with the word "aspic" in it). These guys are terrified of such foods. They seem to think that if they take one bite, they will automatically lose their exploding biceps, develop a lisp, and have to get their hair permed by a guy named Mr. Randi in a screaming-pink salon.

Feed these guys only foods high in fats and cholesterol, like jacuzzi fat-fried cheese sticks and extra greasy Western omelettes served with a couple of Marlboros crushed in the yolk. These guys never worry about their cholesterol or lipid counts. The only count that matters to them is their sperm count. And never wanting to be accused of being the tiniest bit "unmanly" in any area, these men routinely work out in the gym with the Nautilus Groin machine. To keep their buns looking great in their tight jean workclothes, they'll do so many squat thrusts in a day that their butt cheeks will be able to catch a fastball from across the room.

Since the Blue Collar worker has a routine work-day, it's pretty easy to spend romantic evenings at home. Creatures of habit, these 9 to 5 men are very easy to please in bed if you are aware of a few little quirks they share in their sexual attitudes:

1. They like to punch a *timecard* before and after sex.

2. They like to punch *you* before and after sex.

3. When sex is great, they like to smoke a tree afterwards.

4. They keep their marital aids handy in their Sears tool belt worn around their waist at all times.

5. They'll rig up your vibrator with Heavy Duty 24 Volt batteries they borrowed from the offshore drilling platform they're currently working.

6. They like rough foreplay often involving motor oil, a jackhammer, and assorted hydraulic pleasure enhancers.

7. They are romantics, however. They enjoy feeling a soft breeze wafting across their bodies when they make love. So be sure and keep the windows in the pickup truck rolled down.

8. They prefer to "do it" in the truck because objects in the mirror appear larger than they really are.

9. When they get turned on intellectually their brain becomes hard as a rock.

10. They use steel-belted condoms for greater traction.

And for those gals who think that snaring a professional man will get you a lot further down the road than your blue collared cutie's pickup truck can take you, just read on for some real eye openers...

SECTION B: THE WHITE COLLAR HUSBAND

THE DOCTOR HUSBAND: LICENSED TO KILL (You)

These men are interesting studies because they are two completely different personalities before and after they become labeled as a "professional" person. In college and medical school, these guys were considered the prototypes of the universally recognized *mega-nerd*. This is the type of guy who wore such a huge bow tie, you could see it from behind. While everyone else was out partying their brains out, these guys were *in* studying their brains out. Most of them never actually had a date until they got out of their medical internships. On many a lonely Saturday night, they wouldn't *take* a girl out, they would *tear* one out of a magazine.

However, there were a few docs-in-training who did manage to marry before they got out of med school. And their poor unsuspecting wives had no idea about the hardships in store for them. But the "Med-School Wives" learned to band together, surviving incredible odds to go on and become one of the toughest breeds of female survivors around, with the possible exception of Jessica Hahn and All Head Nurses. But anyway, here's some background information highlighting some common roots which bind this peculiar breed of females together:

1. They all met their husbands in the 3rd grade when they looked like Doogie Howser. They went steady with them ever since until the wedding day when they promised to live in poverty, squalor, and have sex on the rare nights he's not on call. And when they do, they

often have to wake him up in the middle of it to ask him if he's having a good time.

2. They are going to enter into a four-year state of "Medical School Induced Hypochondria" and come down with every symptom of each disease their husbands are currently studying about or treating. And by the way, these conditions are always terminal. Even Oral Roberts won't have the power necessary to heal these women of the variety of diseases they are about to contract.

3. They will bear four kids in four years, and be placed at the mercy of his OB/GYN resident buddies' inexperienced hands. This will mean suffering painful intercourse for years from the effects of bungled episiotomies, not to mention the lifetime of ridicule the kids will have to endure over their bullet shaped heads — acquired from having had bad low forceps deliveries.

4. Their social lives will consist entirely of going to Saturday night potluck dinners with a bunch of other med school couples. These gatherings will find the men huddled on one side of the room discussing who screwed up what patient on that day's rounds. But the most important discussions occur when the group shares their collective knowledge of anatomy, namely, the size of the hooters on every nurse who ever walked down the hospital corridor in the past three years. The women will gather in the kitchen to swap coupons, stories on breast feeding, and the possibility of each others' husbands.

This scenario goes on until he begins private practice and then some startling transformations appear in the man as well as the marriage. He is now in an environment where nurses, patients, and staff are literally kissing his feet and catering to his every whim. As his confidence soars, so will his income. The med school wife will suddenly find herself in a position of great insecurity because she's in an entirely new ballgame where he's got all the bases covered. She will be convinced that he has "outgrown" her as he begins acquiring some new things in his life like:

1. A new "designer" hairdo — coiffed and sprayed to the max. This will replace the old barbershop cuts he used to get from Guido in exchange for a surreptitious prescription of Quell Cream for crabs.

2. A new Mercedes sports coupé with personalized license plates reading "GOD = MD = ME".

3. A rolodex filled with the names of pharmaceutical and medical supply saleswomen ingeniously coded as to how desperately they want to *consummate* a sale.

4. A new *trés chic* wardrobe replacing his former "Sears Men's Department" look. He will trade in those old Basses for Ballys, Cricket Club suits for Canali's, and have the Polo insignia glued on his stethoscope. It is natural for the wife to assume that in the midst of all these trade-ins, she might be next on the list.

5. New respect and deference will be paid him on a daily basis, especially when he is wielding a six inch razor sharp scalpel in his hands. Upon entering a room, people will rush up to him and shake his hand. Some will automatically cough, stick out their tongues, or bend over.

Living with a doctor has its own peculiar set of demands attached to it. These men have usually been surrounded by a medical aura for so long that it is bound to rub off on their day-to-day habits.

Even though most women would think that a doctor's intimate knowledge of the human body would automatically make him a great sexual partner, this is usually not true. There are a few little "sexual quirks" most doctors have that a prospective partner should be aware of:

1. They demand a new sheet of examining paper on the bed each time they want to make love.

2. Most doctor husbands will relate to you better during foreplay if you try to make yourself look like the naked subjects they have seen for years in their medical journals. You can easily accomplish this by placing a strip of black tape across your eyes.

3. If you are making love with an eye doctor, he will frequently stop you mid-sex to ask, "Is it better this way ... or this? First position or second? Better? Worse? Or no difference?"

4. A gynecologist will present a whole new set of problems inherent with the job. Do not be insulted if he takes one look at you naked and:
   a. yawns
   b. reflexively grabs the KY Jelly, or...
   c. asks you to empty your bladder before beginning

5. The proctologist, or "Rear Admiral" as he is known in medical circles, can be a real challenge. Although he often boasts that he likes to "do" 18 holes before lunch on any given day, always proceed with extreme caution before entering into any games with him — especially if he tells you he wants to "scope" you out first.

6. Surgeons make wonderful lovers but from force of habit they will want to remove most of your body hair before they begin.

7. The cardiologist will frequently stop making love at timed intervals to check his own pulse and respiration rate. Always diligent not to place undue stress on his heart muscle, it's a sure bet he won't be overworking any other muscle, either.

8. The anesthesiologist is one doc you'll never be able to remember making love to because he prefers his women like his patients — unconscious. And it's a shame, too, because he should be a master at giving *injections*.

9. The psychiatrist can pose a bit of a problem in that he will always insist on making love on his couch. And after 50 minutes, no matter what stage your sexual activity has progressed to, he will announce, "Your time is up."

10. But the pediatricians ... those are the nice guys. They will always give you a lollipop when they are finished.

THE ATTORNEY HUSBAND:
A REAL CASE STUDY

One thing is for sure when you marry an attorney: Don't even bother to enter into an argument with him — you will NEVER win. After reaching a point of total frustration, you could try slapping him across the face with his foulard tie or stomping on his new wing tips, but then he's got you for assault and battery. No matter what tactic you enlist against this legal eagle, you're going to end up a dead duck.

We're talking about a highly educated man who has obtained his third degree in giving the third degree. Attorneys are a suspicious lot by nature who want to believe the worst about you. So be prepared to be cross-examined as he utilizes every trick he has up his legal briefs. He'll be sniffing through your past like a bloodhound, digging out more dirt than you could find under Melvin Belli's fingernails. And no matter how innocent you are, he'll try and find you guilty of *something*. So be smart and take the fifth to avoid innocent remarks being turned into major inquisitions — like the following scenario:

He: "Tell me darling, I'm just curious about something. How many men did you sleep with before you met me?"

She: "I've never been with another man, dear."

He: "You were careful to use the phrase 'been with,' my sweet. This is clearly an admission that you have had sex with other men, though.'

She: "I'm not admitting anything of the sort, counselor."

He: "You are inferring by not admitting to it that you have done it, my slut — er... my sweet."

She: "No — but I *am* inferring that you are acting like a horse's ass, you sleazebag."

He: "These delaying tactics are getting tiresome, you tramp."

She: "So what do you want me to say? I've slept with 100 men before I met you?"

He: "Ah ha! The truth is out; I rest my case."

She: "Okay, you're right. I confess. I've had hundreds of them — and right in your courtroom, too. In fact, I've tried more men than Judge Wapner."

That should rip it. There's nothing like hitting below his Hermes leather belt with a few of your own courtroom tactics to teach him a lesson in your own style of jurisprudence.

LEGAL LOVEMAKING

Like everything else in this legal union, he is not the easiest man to reach an agreement with about anything. Trying to establish a great sex life can be most trying because the lawyer has certain ingrained attitudes from years of courtroom activity. He's a man who has got to be in charge in the courtroom *and* in the bedroom. Here's a few of the stumbling blocks you can expect to encounter when engaged in lovemaking:

1. If you assume a certain position during intercourse, he will automatically take the opposite one.

2. Getting him heated up can pose a problem because he hates to take off his legal briefs.

3. He'll charge you for every 15 minutes of conversation he engages in during foreplay.

4. If you criticize any of his techniques, he'll accuse you of subpoena envy.

5. He does not believe in simultaneous orgasms; the reasoning behind this being that two wrongs don't make a right.

6. He will get the ultimate sexual turn on by asking you to make love on a bench clad only in a black satin robe and powdered peruke. Then afterwards, you must pronounce sentence on his courtroom performance.

7. He gets off on specialized pleasure enhancers like a battery-powered gavel.

8. He'll try to maneuver you into situations that are legally binding — with leather straps.

9. He will insist that you outline your sexual requests on a yellow legal pad and he will take them under advisement.

10. Then, after you've made a formal request for your favorite position, he'll make you plea bargain for it.

* * *

While there are a lot of other professional men such as accountants, clerics, educators, bankers and the like, it would be repetitive and boring to discuss them. This is because in my unbiased opinion — they are all the same under the sheets. If you've seen one white collar guy naked, you've seen them all.

Whether you choose the guy in the blue collar or the white as your mate for life doesn't really matter, because the bottom line is the same — you'll still be scrubbing the dirt off the collars of their shirts every week — only in different colors. And this is what it really all boils down to anyway, isn't it gals? It all comes out in the wash.

QUIZ II

1. The blue collar husband frequents the kind of macho bars where they:
   a. crush beer kegs on their foreheads for fun
   b. laugh until beer shoots out of their noses
   c. look at tarts, throw darts, and pass farts
   d. check their automatic weapons at the door

   * all of the above make for a great night of entertainment

2. The blue collar husband is deathly afraid of:
   a. hair mousse
   b. interior decorators named Quentin
   c. deodorant
   d. three-piece suits

   * d — unless they are made of denim with a leather vest

3. Do not attempt making love to an accountant without:
   a. getting a receipt
   b. removing his pin-striped underwear
   c. bolting his swivel chair to the floor
   d. itemizing your planned activities

   * d — service oriented acts are 20% deductible

4. An OB/GYN husband's idea of making kinky love is to throw you on the sheets and:
   a. tie your hands
   b. tie your feet
   c. tie your legs to the stirrups
   d. tie your tubes

   * c then d

5. The surgeon husband will utilize O.R. protocol when making love by insisting on wearing his:
   a. surgical gloves
   b. surgical condoms
   c. surgical leiderhosen
   d. surgical mask and/or tongue condom

   * *all of the above — which he wears in surgery anyway*

6. The most effective way to make love to a lawyer is by:
   a. finding a loophole
   b. taking the law into your own hands
   c. standing your ground
   d. offering him a generous retainer

   * *b — if that doesn't work try d*

7. What Latin phrase would an attorney most likely whisper during the throes of passionate love-making?
   a. Move your corpus delecti
   b. Get a load of this subpoena
   c. I'd like to get ipso factoed
   d. Where should I file this corpus erectus?

   * *b — make sure it's hand delivered*

CHAPTER 3

THE YOUNG AND THE RESTLESS vs. THE OLD AND LETHARGIC:

The Younger
vs.
The Older Husband From Hell

SECTION A: THE YOUNG HUSBAND

We are all aware that there are a lot of women who do not do the conventional thing by marrying somebody in the same age group as themselves. Actually, some do not marry within the same species as themselves, either, but that's another chapter. Women have the choice in this day and age to marry at either end of the spectrum: choose the excitement of a young stud or the comfort of an old one who has been put out to pasture. It is not only socially acceptable nowadays, but considered quite chic to be seen on the arm of a dashing younger male — one in uniform is especially attractive (sporting his badges and compass) — rather than a man who is so old he remembers the Dead Sea when it was only sick. Let's take a look at the reasons behind these choices, and see what motivates women to cross the age barrier.

THE YOUNGER HUSBAND: COLLEGIATE COUPLING

Even 10 years ago, it was considered shocking to marry, much less be seen with, a younger man. Now, thanks to the examples set by aging starlets with alleged great quantities of plastic surgically implanted in their bodies like Cher and Mary Frann, it has become the "in" thing to snag your own personal Ken doll. You know — the type that has blow-dried hair and the attention span of an Irish Setter. It's perfectly okay to have a strapping young man who will fulfill your womanly desires. You don't have to make excuses anymore about him being your "intellectual equal." Nobody is going to believe you picked him for his IQ anyway, which incidentally is usually the same as a slice of toast.

Young husbands are fun to have around because of their playful natures. And lucky for you that many of them learned their play skills at the Rob Lowe Day Care Center. If you just happened to snatch one straight out of college, life can be a continual party. But you must be cautioned about the kinds of pranks you might fall victim to from your "party hearty" honey...

It will not be unusual for you to get into a bed that has been shortsheeted on a nightly basis. Or, to be mooned whenever you enter the room. Or have to watch him practice his collegiate favorite — bending over with a match and having a continual blue flame of gas shooting out of his butt. Now there's a skill that will surely come in handy later in life.

But these guys are so easy going it makes it all worthwhile. All they have known is dorm life for the past few years, so you won't have to do much to keep them happy. They have a minimal amount of needs that you can fulfill with no effort at all — besides they're cheap to keep. Here's a few of your college man's minimum daily requirements:

1. He is used to group showers in the gym. So invite some of his fraternity brothers over, get a "soap on a rope," and you can all pile into the shower together and sing "Hail To Sigma Chi" at the top of your lungs. And just to make all the guys feel at home, between songs roll up your towel and snap them on their behinds.

2. His most complicated gourmet request will be to add sauteed onions to his hamburger. This should not pose a major problem, because the cooks at Burger King are only too happy to do it his way.

3. There is no need to buy a King or Queen bed for the two of you. Since he got all his sexual

experience on a dorm cot, he'll be totally used to — in fact, prefer — a twin bed with a sagging mattress, squeaking springs, and sheets dirty enough to spontaneously combust.

4. He is easy to get rid of if you want a night out with the girls or just to spend time alone. Simply say to him, "Isn't there a Porky's Film Festival you should be attending tonight?" And he's outta there. Works like a charm every time.

5. Conversation is no chore with these men-in-training. They are only interested in two topics: sex and football, so you can kill two birds with one stone. Frequently pepper your conversation during sexual foreplay with phrases like, "Honey, that TIGHT END is your best position — so give it to me while your BACKFIELD'S IN MOTION — because I don't mind doing that ILLEGAL PROCEDURE to you — baby, as long as you COMPLETE THAT PASS for me."

THE HIGH SCHOOL HONEY:
AN ELEMENTARY EDUCATION

You may want to go even younger. One advantage of really young guys is that they are not set in their ways and enjoy sharing wonderful moments with you that you had long forgotten — like making out in the movies or going to fun events like carnivals, picnics, and hayrides. But there is a down side, too. You'll have to keep in mind that there's going to be some things you really won't feel like sharing with him — like his high school graduation, Senior Prom, and teenage acne flareups. But these things are a small sacrifice considering the intense pleasures you'll be sharing together.

Be prepared for your friends alluding that "all relationships with immature men are only based on physical attraction." Tell them that you have a news flash for them: it's not such a bad idea, they ought to try it! Then add that no guy ever reaches a point of total maturity. So this time around, you finally got smart and saved yourself all those years of waiting for your man to grow up — you went straight for the young dude in the first place.

The young guys are into leather clothes in a big way. They love wearing black leather jackets and matching tight black leather pants. In fact, when they wear this kind of ensemble, they are frequently mistaken for garment bags at airports, so you have to keep a close eye on them. At other times, the teenage guy loves to wear those revealing muscle T-shirts which leave you feeling weak at the sight of his biceps. And how about the sight of those sweet tight buns in a pair of Levi 501 jeans? This certainly is not hard on the eyes considering that your last husband was so fat he had to stuff his flabby butt into 1002's.

PUBESCENT PASSIONS

The main advantage of the teenage mate can be summed up in one word: STAMINA. These guys are like magnificent stallions, whereas the older men can't even get out of the gate half of the time. But don't let your jealous girlfriends try to give you any crap about "you're only in the relationship for the sex." Insist it's not true. There's a lot more to a teenage guy than being your own personal stud horse. And if you think about it for a few days, you just might be able to come up with one or two. The fact is, there are many physical activities not involving sex that these fine young men will have you become willing participants in...

1. Mud wrestling in the nude.
2. The new dynamic sport of Bedspring Olympics.
3. A grueling hour of "One-on-One" — followed by some basketball.
4. Two hours of Ice Hockey — as a warm-up exercise for three hours of Tongue Hockey.
5. And for the truly game, you can always participate in one of his favorite track and field events like Pole Vaulting. This will make him so happy, he will return the favor by giving his all with a private demonstration of the Broad Jump.

You'll find that having a young stud around the house will definitely add new dimensions to your life. You'll have the new-found energy to do so many things at once; whereas with your former husband you had difficulty doing even two things at the same time — such as having sex and enjoying yourself.

* * *

However, there's still a large segment of the female population who are definitely not into cradle robbing. They're into, shall we say, grave robbing. This is where the older husband comes into the picture. Many women prefer the more stable relationship an older man can offer. A man who has both feet planted firmly on the ground. Or in some cases, a well-heeled older gentleman with one foot on the ground and the other in a kicking stance close to the bucket. In any case, let's see what the future (however short it may be) can hold with the older husband from hell...

SECTION B: THE OLD HUSBAND

THE OLDER HUSBAND: YOUR BEST INVESTMENT

Younger women marry older men for a *variety* of reasons. In fact, there doesn't seem to be a common thread when one examines the motivations behind this particular choice. She may be looking for:

1. A father figure — *with lots of bucks*
2. An experienced lover — *with lots of bucks*
3. A man who no longer desires children — *with lots of bucks*
4. A man who has risen to the top echelons in his field — *with lots of bucks*
5. A man possessing the wisdom and maturity lacking in younger men — *with lots of bucks*

See? It is difficult to choose any one particular reason given so variable a field. Let's just say that some women are looking for a man they can really bank on.

GETTING IT ON WITH ONE WHO IS GETTING ON

In the area of making love, the older man can be as exciting as the younger man if you know what to expect. However, you will have to make a few allowances for the older husband in order to increase his pleasure. And speaking of allowances — *yours* can be increased by at least $100 per week if you do certain things for him. So read carefully:

1. He reached his sexual peak 20 years ago, while you are just reaching yours — so it can get lonely on the top. Slow down and don't burn

his gears out — keep him properly oiled and lubricated.

2.   The older man adores the fact that he is able to make love with a younger woman. It makes him feel like an adventurer. In fact, one might call him the *bald adventurer*. And to reinforce that image, he loves to watch his performance in a room filled with mirrors. This can be an added boon to the wife who wishes to monitor his state of health during rigorous sexual romps. Keep a small mirror of your own in hand and put it under his nose at various intervals to make sure he's still breathing.

3.   Older men may take a little longer to get aroused — say, a day and a half — so you must be very patient. And learning the art of taking quick five-minute naps doesn't hurt either.

4.   Some older men use amyl nitrate to enhance their staying power during lovemaking. You might want to substitute some nitroglycerin to make sure he's "staying alive."

5.   Older men are totally straight forward with you about what they expect from your lovemaking. And the one thing they don't want you to do is make them Daddies at their advanced age. Of course, this should be no problem because the older man, while he not only shoots straight from the hip, he usually shoots blanks, too.

DRESSING FOR RETIREMENT

Younger women often admire an older man's finely developed sense of style in his attire, which he has carefully cultivated over the years. Most of them have become comfortable in wearing traditional dark-colored tailored suits and the finest Sea Isle cotton custom made shirts with the monogrammed cuff. They gravitate toward fine silk ties with matching silk pocket squares which cut a very stunning figure, indeed. They are meticulous in choosing calf-length dark silk socks which fit perfectly under the beautiful Ferragamo shoes they've become accustomed to ordering direct from Italy. They keep their distinguished gray hair short, scrupulously clean, and professionally coiffed. And they are fastidious about keeping their entire person clean, well-pressed, and tidy.

But there is an age somewhere around the mid 60's when these same men will one day wake up and abruptly forget all of these fine grooming habits acquired over the years. They will have literally metamorphosized overnight from the epitome of great fashion taste to looking like they have purchased their entire wardrobe from a thrift shop. This is when the man you have always thought of as "the silver fox" exits and is replaced by his new alter-ego "the mangy dog." No one is sure why this happens but be assured that it does. At this point you'll be able to officially classify the older man in your life as a "Geezer." You can immediately identify the *Geeze State* by:

1. His polyester golf pants in an array of colors including shell pink, saffron yellow, lime green, and piquant puce. Please note that he never wears them with a shirt that even remotely goes with the pants. The shirts are always of a contrasting pattern, color, and two sizes too big or small.

2. The geeze will develop an inexplicable penchant for the Ferdinand Marcos-type shirts that do not have to be tucked inside his pants. His new shirts are the kind that are hemmed eight inches below the waist and have a zipper front closing. They also do a completely miserable job of hiding his ever-expanding gut. But he is proud of this new look, telling everyone that he had them custom made overseas. The sad truth is that he purchased them from vendors on every street corner in Tijuana, Mexico.

3. The Ferragamos have been forever replaced by sandals but the socks remain calf length — only this time they are black cotton. Naturally they are always worn with plaid shorts.

4. Other shirts are worn with the top buttons always fastened while the bottom two remain open. The rest of the shirt is stretched tightly across his chest, gaping open just enough to reveal three extra-long gray chest hairs.

5. His choice of sport jacket is always in the red-orange range of plaid and made from triple-ply polyester capable of stopping bullets from an M-16. He can sleep, swim, sweat, or build a house in it without ever showing a trace of a wrinkle.

6. The silver hair becomes increasingly yellowed, unkempt, and too sparse to warrant any kind of coif. Naturally, the part begins just over the left ear, and the few thinning strands are combed over the bald head and end someplace below the right rear. Some older men even opt for the discount hair transplant which leaves

the conspicuous Frankenstein stitch scars prominently displayed mid forehead.

7. You will have a record of everything he's eaten for the past month, because there will be assorted dried morsels of it on his ties.

8. For no apparent reason, he will henceforth never be seen without a hat. It will be felt; he'll wear it in 100 degree temperatures and gale-force winds — it will become an integral part of his persona.

9. Contrary to the natural laws of gravity, his waist is now located ten inches higher than it was last year. This means that now his belt buckle will be located somewhere in the middle of his chest.

10. Leather shoes are now a thing of the past with The Geeze. On the rare days when he is not wearing his sandals, he has gravitated to the spit n' wipe vinyl types — chosen in his favorite colors, daffodil yellow and year 'round Clorox white. These are prominently featured at blue light specials and held together at the heels by that tough plastic string. And apparently, most of them forget to cut it — which explains that slow, halting gait.

DRIVING US CRAZY

Remembering how to dress is not the only thing the older husband will abruptly forget. The next thing to go is his driving skills. Even if he was as slick as Sterling Moss in his younger days, he will develop some pretty horrific driving habits in his later years. How does this happen? Many women believe that all older husbands must sneak off to

Florida for a week and enroll themselves in an intensive course on "How To Drive Like The World's Oldest Geeze." There they receive on-the-road experience from the world's only brain-dead driving instructor, named Manny. Among their more memorable moves guaranteed to give you a premature heart attack are:

1. The gut wrenching stunt of making a left turn across three lanes of traffic from the right lane (while signalling a right turn with his flasher). This is a maneuver pioneered by Manny himself, and faithfully executed by every man over the age of 60 who is licensed to drive in the state of Florida. In fact, Manny requires that all his men be able to do this routinely before they can pass his course and return to their home state.

2. Driving with his felt hat pulled down over his ears, smoking a smelly cigar, with the seat lowered to where he can't see over the steering wheel and has to look through it. This necessitates a restricted license, requiring him to be accompanied by a seeing-eye dog in the front seat at all times for consultation.

3. Never stopping to ask for directions — even when hopelessly lost. He will start out for the shopping mall in suburban Maryland and end up in Grants Pass, Oregon, four days later, still refusing to ask a service station attendant for directions.

4. He will use his signal lights in a new way from now on. The plan is to signal, and then change lanes immediately without checking his rear or

sideview mirrors, no matter where any other vehicles are positioned on the road.

5. Because of his impaired driving ability, he will become so expert at taking highway abuse from other motorists that he will be the inspiration for a new defensive driver's manual called "Finger Gestures For The Open Road."

6. He always parks illegally — everywhere. This is because he refuses to walk any further than one foot to get anyplace. This man is so lazy that he will eventually end up with the ultimate traffic ticket — for illegally parking in a handicapped bathroom stall.

7. Prone to falling asleep at stoplights, he will force other motorists to get caught for no less than three light changes. And then he can't figure out why everyone is pointing at him with their middle fingers.

8. He will adopt the all-important Old Timer's Two Foot Rule: one foot on the gas and the other foot on the brake at all times.

9. At any busy intersection when executing a left hand turn, he will always put on his right hand turn signal, close his eyes, hit the gas, pray and go like hell.

10. He will never exceed the standard speed limit for geezes, 34 m.p.h. — especially when driving on any major freeway. He will have at least 4 semi's and 6 RV's tailgating him for 3 hours as the drivers keep re-loading their rifles in an attempt to pick him off.

* * *

So there you have it. Life with husbands from opposite ends of the time warp — and make no mistake about it; *you* will emerge warped in either case. But hey, it's okay. Who ever said life had to be lived on the straight and narrow? In a nutshell:

"Young studs are the spice of life and old geezers the saltpeter. How you want to shake it is strictly up to you."

QUIZ III

1. The biggest problem the old geeze husband has is:
   a. getting himself dressed
   b. getting his dentures to fit
   c. getting his walker into the car
   d. getting it up

   * b — *if he can find them*

2. One reason a young woman marries an older man is because:
   a. she wants a father figure
   b. she's always wanted to live in St. Petersburg
   c. she really digs those Depends
   d. she doesn't like sex very much

   * a — *like Father Time*

3. Your experience can be of invaluable help to the younger husband with:
   a. his maturation process
   b. his financial development
   c. his appreciation of the finer things of life
   d. his homework

   * d — *especially in Sex Ed.*

4. Which of the following is considered to be a marital aid by the older husband?
   a. an oxygen mask
   b. a hydraulic Foley catheter
   c. a feather-lined hernia truss
   d. tequila and prune juice shooters laced with Spanish Fly

   * b — *works exceptionally well with d in the IV bag*

5. Which of the following is considered to be a marital aid by the younger husband?
   a. Levi's 501 condoms
   b. a 2 Live Crew concert tape
   c. a leather Harley Davidson used biker seat
   d. a Timex stopwatch

   * d — *like him, it'll take a lickin' but keep on tickin'*

CHAPTER 4

HIS ILLNESSES ARE KILLING YOU:

The Hypochondriac Husband From Hell vs. The Healthy Wife

[YOUR PICTURE HERE]

SECTION A: THE HEALTHY WIFE

We women don't have to prove a thing when it comes to showing how physically tough we are, because our track records speak for themselves. The *fairer sex* can be found matriculating in our country's most prestigious diesel academies, pumping iron in the gym, and delivering our own babies in the back of a cab while the male driver has passed out cold from the sight. We have to be strong because we are the nurturers and caretakers of the family. Without our constant care, the whole family unit would be wearing two different colored socks and mismatched shoes every day of the week — not to mention subsisting on Twinkies for breakfast, lunch, and dinner. This being the case, there is just no room in a woman's life to take a day off and be sick — we are on call 24 hours a day. Sickness is a luxury that women can't afford.

STAND AND DELIVER

There is only one event in a woman's life that used to give us about a week's respite — and that was when we checked into the hospital to have a baby. But the bad news is that nowadays those *wonderful* folks at the Big Medical Insurance Company which shall remain nameless (but rhymes with "Glue Floss") will not allow us to stay in the hospital for more than three days — labor time included. So after an agonizing 36 hour labor and delivery, including an episiotomy the size of the Grand Canyon, they will send a representative into the delivery room with your packed suitcase as the last stitch is going in. And within five minutes after you have delivered the afterbirth, you are history. Long gone are the days when we had a week to relax in the hospital bed, being totally pampered before we had to go home and *face the music* — which in our case is, "I Haven't Got Time For The Pain."

If you are having your first baby, you should be aware that, once you get home, you will have barely dragged your butt and your new baby over the threshold when your well-intentioned husband will utter these fateful words:

"Honey, I know you need your rest, and you can count on me to help out all I can — *but first* there's a few things I absolutely must do right now."

Watch out! This statement is a dead giveaway that within the next five seconds, you will hear the sound of his car burning rubber as it leaves the driveway at 60 m.p.h. You will not see his face again for at least a week. You will be left alone, just minutes into your post-partum depression, to run the household with no help whatsoever.

But rest assured that while you're functioning as a Spike Jones one-woman band having all your body parts in use at the same time between diapering, singing lullabyes, breastfeeding, rocking, burping, walking, etc., he will be attending to his own "high priority items" — items SO IMPORTANT, in his opinion, that if they're not accomplished within the hour, the entire structure of the nuclear family unit could immediately disintegrate. Well, ladies, get wise to his evasive game plan — and fast!! This behavior is common to all new Dads who have been alone all week while you were in the hospital delivering that precious cargo. These guys want NO part of the grueling stuff ahead — kids crying, poopy diapers, 2 a.m. feedings, and your complaining! So now that you're back home to take over, he is free to take off and accomplish all those vital errands he's allegedly doing "just for you."

1. His first stop is a crucial visit to the Hardware Store where he will spend the entire afternoon fondling every size of nail, bolt, and variety of spackling compound manufactured in the free world. Women will never be able to understand what kind of macho turn-on hardware has for the men in their lives, but suffice it to say, they can get as hot over wire, tools, and the smell of paint thinner as they can over an X-rated movie.

2. Next, he will check into the local Unisex Salon to get his hair coiffed, blow-dried, and sprayed into a perfect lacquered shell by a buxom operator named Cyndi who wears black fishnet stockings and a styrofoam padded push-up bra. (This will be followed by an erotic two-hour manicure and cuticle massage that will literally set his socks on fire.) Be advised that the next time you see him, the effect will make him look like he's wearing Lee Press-On hair.

3. The next few days will be filled with the "Marathon Car Wash" itinerary. He will order "the works" — which includes the super Carnuba waxing process (one week), the major interior steam cleaning renewal system complete with carpet and dashboard revitalization and the optional "real leather" spray simulation (12 hours 13 minutes), plus the extensive wire wheel brush cleaning and grease removing

process (up to $1^1/_2$ days). It goes without saying that he will feel the need to personally supervise every step of each operation, including the wax drying process which takes place in the newly constructed Far East Typhoon Wind Tunnel where hot air jets of 230 m.p.h. are funneled directly upon him riding in the car with the top down. But rest assured even this gale force will be unable to ruffle one hair on his newly shellacked head.

4. Then it's an absolute necessity on his agenda that he shop for socks. Even though the ones in his sock drawer are multiplying at a rate greater than the population of Bangladesh, men always panic when they get down to their last 60 pairs. This is probably because approximately 95% of the pairs do not match each other. They blame it on your washing machine which accepts them in pairs, but at the end of the spin cycle mysteriously gives back only one of each set. Now, this *is* universally true no matter what brand of washer you have. We women can attest to it as gospel. But what we do not understand is why men spend more time and energy agonizing over choosing sock colors to exactly match their pants, but not be the least bit bothered by the fact that their toupees don't even come close to matching their hair.

5. And last but not least, he must attend the one event in his life that even death could not stop — his poker game. This is an integral part of how a man maintains his masculinity. It is the one place where he can smoke cigars, talk big,

cuss, and smear onion dip on his pants in an atmosphere of total acceptance and unconditional love. Ladies, wouldn't you agree this touching moment deserves a Hallmark sensitivity card?

Any woman who has children will attest to this: when a new mother comes home from the hospital with her new baby, she can look forward to her husband being on a continual "important errand run," lasting roughly until the baby is either potty trained or walking — whichever comes last. But wait ... there's more. The next event we can look forward to, for racking up enough legal points to qualify for total desertion, is when we get the flu.

SICKNESS: NOT ON HIS TIME

Remember that part of the old marriage vow, "In sickness and in health ... 'til death do us part?" Any bed-ridden wife will agree that, more accurately, it should be, "'Til flu do us part."

A sick woman is out of luck. There is just no time in her busy life to stay in bed and get well. How many of us have woken up with a 105 degree temp, aching muscles, and splitting headache and recited all our symptoms to a sympathetic husband? Dream on. By the time we get to the second symptom of vertigo and nausea, he's in the shower. Do we really expect to be "excused" for the day? No damn way. We'd have better odds of getting excused from jury duty on a capital offense case. Get used to the idea that you're going to have to do all of your usual chores plus much, much more. So here's some survival tips to help you get through the day when every minute feels like it's going to be your last:

1. Drive to the nearest *fast fix* medical clinic like the corner "Doc-in-the-Box" for prompt treatment. Actually, even these take too long if the treatment plan is more than fifteen minutes. What we really need is a Drive-In Medical McClinic where you can recite your symptoms into a microphone to the short order doc on call. In seconds, he will dispense your antibiotic to you in a paper bag through the drive-in service window, but not before asking, "You want a Pap smear with that?"

2. Take quick naps between laundry cycles, putting your head in the cold water rinse periodically to keep from passing out altogether. Try a liberal application of Downy, too, which will soften up those tense, aching muscles.

3. When your temperature goes down to 103 degrees, be prepared for your husband to assume that you have spontaneously undergone an Earnest Angley Miracle Cure. He will then insist that for your continued well-being, exercise is a must. Therefore, you need to engage in a much-needed lovemaking marathon with him for the rest of the evening. It seems there is not a man on earth who does not truly believe in his heart that making love is the cure for any illness or problem life throws your way. Your weakened state could be the same as if you had just gone 15 rounds with Mike Tyson and your husband will insist on making love right after the last punch has landed.

4. The *minute* you recognize flu symptoms coming on, go to the Deli and stock up on prepared dinner items. You can bet your life that during

a bout with the flu, your husband will decide *now's* the time to invite his corporate superiors over for a lengthy five-course sit-down dinner. He will call you at 3 p.m. and tell you that he does not want to put any pressure on you while you're under the weather, but your entire futures are riding on the success of this dinner party.

5. Install a porta-john in the back of your station wagon. Diarrhea waits for no one. With carpools, grocery shopping, and PTA, you'll be on the road for eight hours straight without a pit stop. And even if you should find yourself a participating service station willing to give you the key to the bathroom, by the time you circle the building eight times trying to find where it is, it'll be too late.

6. He will beg you to get up off your deathbed to "just spend five minutes at my mother's in honor of her birthday." And here's the totally predictable part, ladies. He will swear on a stack of Bibles that all you will need to do is just run in for a minute and say "Hi," and then you can both leave. To insure your survival, you'd better learn to give him an unequivocal "No." Because the reality of the situation is that if you agree to go, there's no way you'll be leaving before *five* hours. And as your fever is escalating, so is his blood alcohol level from his fifth scotch and water. Six hours later, the paramedics will be called in to transport *both* of you out of the house on stretchers.

SECTION B:
THE HYPOCHONDRIAC HUSBAND

THE COMMON COLD: Rx DEATH WARRANT FOR ALL MALES

There is only one thing more sure than death and paying taxes and that's when the hypochondriac husband gets even so much as the sniffles, he will regress even beyond acting like an infant. He will be as totally helpless as a fetus.

The hypochondriac husband, always on the alert for the Grim Reaper, will self-diagnose to the point where a minor sore throat is considered terminal cancer. He will immediately take to his bed with a case of Kleenex, assume the fetal position, cancel all activities that involve walking, and self-medicate for a period of not less than five days until he reaches the clinical state of "stupor." You will then assume full household responsibilities and have to wear two hats:

a. The Maintenance Hard Hat — as the head of the household you will now have to assume his *one* official duty of changing fuses.

b. The Nurse's Cap — as you step into the role of Florence Nightingale, you must be careful not to miss administering any of his medications — plus, take halfhourly temperature readings, and carry enough water to his bedside to support a flotilla. And as if this wasn't bad enough, you must assume your best bedside manner and listen to him whine through his list of complaints, remembering to pat his hand and nod at regular intervals (trying not to nod off) — all the while wearing an expression of great sympathy.

ANATOMICAL ALIBIS

The hypochondriac husband is capable of developing symptoms to any one of hundreds of Major Diseases at a moment's notice. Upon discovering one, he will pull out his autographed copy of the Merck Manual (which he carries around at all times), look it up, and interpret each symptom as proof he has contracted one of the most arcane diseases ever discovered. For him, timing is crucial here because a fatal disease is certainly just cause to get out of some occasions just too painful to endure. Here are some classic situations he will avoid by "spontaneously generating" at least one symptom of a major disease:

1.   The Family Reunion.

This event will trigger malaise, fever, and instant irritability in the heretofore able-bodied husband. He will insist on a minimum isolation period of 48 hours (Saturday-Sunday) until the imminent danger of having to socialize with all the geeky relatives has passed.

2.   Traveling In and Out Of Airports.

The hypochondriac will develop the world's fastest case of a bad back within seconds of pulling up to the terminal. As he is bent over in acute pain clutching his sacroiliac, *you* will be lifting the eight pieces of matching luggage out of the car trunk, and dragging them into the terminal by yourself. Simultaneously, you will also have to juggle a baby, three diaper tote bags, push the stroller with your teeth across the parking lot and dodge gypsy cabs — while he manages (with a great show of pain) to carry your wallet for you.

While bad backs are an elusive condition that are capable of being undetected by an MRI scan, be assured that one will inevitably flare up in the face of any of the following stimuli:

a. *Furniture that needs to be moved.*

Forget it. Unless it's down-stuffed futons or the glue-together brand of furniture made from balsa, there won't be any strapping man around to hoist something like your grandmother's old chest. (He might be able to move *yours,* but that's another story.) The only thing "strapping" around your house will be what's done *to* you — as he graciously offers to tie your armoire onto your back so you can carry it across the room.

b. *Grocery bags in the back of the station wagon.*

Women have been known to pull up to the front door loaded with 30 bags of groceries in their hatchbacks expecting their husbands to come out and help carry them inside. Six hours later, the bags remain untouched. The only living things on the scene will be the 6,000 buzzing flies attracted by the stench of overripe cantaloupes and the gooey river of melted ice cream on the carpet. When you discover this smoldering compost heap is still in the back of your car, he will, in response to your bloodcurdling screams, reluctantly come out and carry the bag of paper towels into the house. Then he will disappear off to the gym and spend the next three hours bench-pressing iron equivalent in tonnage to the Exxon Valdez.

3.   All the other jobs a woman needs help with from shampooing the cat, dog, or carpet to re-potting ficus trees.

These are all skillfully avoided as the hypochondriac husband develops job-specific allergies. Allergies are a dandy excuse because they can come and go when convenient to the "aller-gee." And they sound so convincing, too. Oft elicited responses to your requests for help range from, "I'd love to help shampoo Cujo, Darling. But you know I have an allergy to Pit Bull dander from the canine metatarsal," to "Honey, not the ficus. Last time I touched it, the chlorophyll made my brain stem swell."

You could advise him that if he doesn't help you he might suffer a more severe reaction than a swollen brain. Namely, a swollen lip in response to your fist. But then it would mean sinking to his level, and that's a hell of a long way down.

PREVENTATIVE MEDICINE

The hypochondriac is always on the alert to avoid any situation where he might possibly encounter some renegade germs. This means that within 24 hours of the kids returning from their Equal Opportunity Viral Daycare Center, he will isolate himself from them for fear of being contaminated with chicken pox, measles, whooping cough, or whatever "virus of the day" is being passed from kid to kid through the vehicle of shared drool and nose snot over their Spaghetti-O's.

So to insure a germfree environment, you not only need to add a half-gallon of Clorox to the rinse cycle, but your husband will insist you throw in the clothes with the kids still in them.

SUFFERING IN SILENCE FOR THE GIPPER

It is interesting to note that the hypochondriac will choose to ignore *truly serious* symptoms when they manifest themselves during any sporting event. He will happily sit through a four-hour football game without acknowledging some major league symptoms like tightness in the chest, sweating, nausea, and pain radiating down his right arm — until the last second of the fourth quarter. These are minor inconveniences that he will chalk up to "easily explainable" causes like *the humidity* and *the six moss-covered hotdogs* he just wolfed down in one bite. It is only when the other fans are leaving the stadium that he will call for an oxygen mask, because he's too weak to get up off the bleachers.

A LITTLE KNOWLEDGE IS A DANGEROUS THING

Armed with a little medical knowledge (and may I stress *very little*) they have acquired throughout their lifetime of near death experiences, the hypochondriac will automatically assume the worst given any symptom. Women are used to having husbands jump to the following ridiculous conclusions given the ordinary aches and pains we all abide at one time or another. The trick here is to not get sucked into his neuroses. Just humor him when the following situations come up:

1. HEADACHE

To a hypochondriac this can mean only one thing: an inoperable brain tumor. But not just your ordinary everyday *garden variety* of inoperable brain tumor. It must be the same kind Bette Davis contracted in "Dark Victory." He will take to lighting two cigarettes at a time (even though he is a non-smoker) and mimicking Bette's vocal intonations while batting his baby blues. He may even go so far as to dramatically address your son by calling out "Peet-ah, Peet-ah, Pee-tah" which is totally absurd because the kid's name is Michael. But humor him. You do not want to come straight out and tell him that he is full of you-know-what. Instead, to drive home your point, tell him you are giving him two Excedrins for the headache and an enema for the relief of his more apparent problem.

2. SWOLLEN GLANDS, SORE THROAT, AND FEVER.

This will positively do him in. Convinced that because of his reckless sexual past, which he has recounted to you more times than you care to remember, he has contracted syphilis and is now presenting with the tertiary stages. He will become more horrified by the second as he remembers the fate encountered by the poor syphilitic P.F.C.'s pecker from the old Army training films he witnessed in his youth. This memory will have him dropping his pants every five minutes to see if *his* has fallen off yet. Here is your perfect opportunity to get back at him for having had to endure years of his highly exaggerated stories about bedding numerous women. Tell him it looks like a terminal case of syphilis to you too, and that the only cure you've ever heard of is surgical removal.

3. DIFFICULTY IN URINATING.

This will immediately convince him that prostate trouble is brewing. After checking out his prostate gland five times daily, he will be positive that it is enlarging at the rate of 5mm. per hour. Assure him that this is pure nonsense — just a figment of his imagination. But tell him what you *don't* understand is why he is carrying around a Casaba melon in his pants.

4. ORDINARY CONSTIPATION.

This will be interpreted to mean he has developed a bowel obstruction the size of Gibraltar. He will aggravate the situation by sending himself into a sphincter spasm from intense worry. After hearing about the state of his bowels for three interminable days and nights, you will have reached your limit. Make him swallow a box of Dulcolax, followed up by a high colonic irrigation. Then push him into the bathroom and immediately take cover in the corner of your basement with the kids and pets. After hearing the sound of porcelain shattering and the rafters shaking, you will know he has been cured and you can come out.

Living with a man who is constantly contracting the Disease-of-the-Week poses special challenges which can only be taken on by the most able bodied woman — or a woman whose vaccinations

73

are up to date — or a woman with a need to punish herself. Your best bet would be to consider entering the medical profession yourself, which in the long haul would save you hundreds of thousands of dollars in medical bills. But more importantly, it might also save a precious *life* — that of your husband's physician — who is seriously considering suicide as a viable alternative to spending the rest of *his* treating your hypochondriac husband.

QUIZ IV

1. As the pregnant wife of a hypochondriac husband who is your labor coach, you can expect to hear the following from him in the labor room:
   a. more moaning and groaning than you're doing
   b. "Nurse, can I have a blindfold?"
   c. silence (i.e., he's passed out)
   d. "Do I have to stick around for the pushing?"

   * d — *and ask the nurse to do everyone a favor and push his butt out of the room*

2. The hypochondriac comes down with severe diarrhea while vacationing in Mexico. You should give him:
   a. Pepto-Bismol
   b. Lomotil
   c. Immodium AD
   d. a cork

   * d — *then cross your fingers, his legs and immediately board a plane for the states*

3. The hypochondriac is terrified about the prospect of his upcoming vasectomy. To sensitively explain the procedure to him, utilize which visual aid:
   a. a weed whacker
   b. a sausage and a meat grinder
   c. a banana and a meat cleaver
   d. a balloon and a hat pin

   * c — *good for circumcision demos, too*

4. The hypochondriac husband reaches his sexual peak:
   a. in his mid-thirties
   b. between illnesses
   c. in the fetal stage
   d. after death

   * d — *where he can stay stiff indefinitely*

5. The hypochondriac may develop a long-term dependency on:
   a. Preparation H
   b. Valium suppositories
   c. Ben Casey reruns
   d. rectal thermometers

   * c — *Ben looks like he is perennially constipated, himself*

CHAPTER 5

IT'S NOT ALWAYS NICE TO HAVE A MAN AROUND THE HOUSE:

The Helpless Husband vs. The Do-It-Yourself Husband From Hell

SECTION A:
THE HELPLESS HUSBAND

THE REVENGE OF MA BELL

We are all brought into this world as helpless newborn babes requiring constant attention from our parents. But at some point in later years, we should finally arrive at a state of independence. What some women did not count on is that once their husbands reach adulthood, many of them actually *regress* to the point where they are about on par with a *fetus* in being able to take care of themselves. These men never truly lose their *umbilical cords* — instead they just hang there and ultimately mutate into a new form of adult lifeline known as the PHONE CORD. The phone becomes an instrument of immediate gratification, and the helpless husband doesn't hesitate to use it any time of day to barrage you with lists of errands he needs done, pose life and death questions he wants answered immediately, or just have the security of knowing where you are and hearing your voice. While he views his phone calls as "absolutely necessary," the wife sees every call as a "necessary evil" — and the telephone becomes the "instrument of the devil" making her life a hell on earth.

She will find that she no longer has the privilege of even five uninterrupted minutes to sit on the john, shave her legs, or have just a moments peace without being called on *her* home phone, from *his* car phone, work phone, or the worst technological invention to date — the airplane phone. These calls are placed at regular half-hour intervals throughout the day by her *well-meaning* husband who claims he is calling just to "touch base." And while the working wife's productivity is cut by at least 40% from his constant calls, his will increase by 80%, because you end up doing his errands instead of your own. Now with the advent of the cellular phone, which many men carry around in their brief-cases or briefs (whichever does it for them), there are no limits. He can reach out and touch you via Ma Bell wherever and whenever he gets the urge. Forget "Women's Lib." We are desperately in need of "Phone Lib," because there will no longer be one solitary place on earth where we can find a safe haven from having our days riddled with constant interruptions from the panicky husband with the following "life or death" requests:

1. Calls home to have you locate the dry cleaning ticket he misplaced approximately three months ago. After ripping the house apart and still unable to find it, you'll probably have to appear at the cleaners rip-roaring drunk and promise the pain-in-the-butt proprietor a lusty romp on the mangler in exchange for your husband's clothes.

2. Calls from his car phone because he's in the mood for a little "phone sex." Tell him that he needs to practice "safe sex." It wouldn't be prudent to have this type of conversation at 60 miles per hour, because he needs to keep both hands on the wheel.

3. Calls for the location of his checkbook. He last remembers putting it in the pocket of his shirt which is currently being pulverized by the

double-duty agitator in your Whirlpool washing machine.

4. Calls during the last exciting three minutes of your favorite soap opera to find out if:
    a. the Evil Twin has murdered the heroine yet
    b. the heroine has delivered her baby after an 18 month pregnancy, culminating in a gut-busting 10 episodes of labor

    Because his phone call made you miss the exciting climax to a six month storyline you've been following daily, get the ultimate revenge by delivering your own news during the last crucial five minutes of the next Laker's game — tell him you're pregnant — with twins.

5. They always seem to call while we're on the john, so that we have to make an awkward mad dash for the phone, with our underpants dangling somewhere around our knees. And just as we answer, he hangs up. Later, you find out he was calling just to see what you were doing. Get smart. You can squelch this kind of call once and for all by describing exactly what you were doing in excruciatingly graphic detail.

6. Calls while you're scrubbing the floor which take up an hour of your time as he recites a list of things you must do for him that day, which include:
    a. buy extra Slim Jims for lunch bag
    b. check level of motor oil in lawn mower
    c. take dog to vet for dental scaling
    d. search through hardware store barrels for obscure sized lug nuts
    e. locate tax returns from years 1978-84
    f. store box of Preparation H in freezer

While writing down the countless the items, you finally lose your composure and threaten that if he gives you one more task, you're going to call up a guy named "Vinnie" who will "reach out and *touch*" both of his knee caps.

7. Calls in a panic from the airline phone somewhere over Cleveland to report that he is close to death from airline food poisoning, and he has filled his barf bag beyond the recommended safety limits.

Or when he's at home and needs immediate assistance, he'll spend hours tracking you down all over town:

1. Has you paged in the grocery store to tell you he is looking for a can of soup but doesn't know where the pantry is located in the house.

2. Calls you on the cellular phone as you are being wheeled into the delivery room to ask why the washing machine is regurgitating large quantities of suds when he only used half-a-box of Tide.

3. Calls you at the beauty parlor because he can't find the remote control for the TV — and doesn't know which button on the set turns it on.

Ironically, this is the same guy who apparently does not know how to answer a ringing telephone. Instead, he becomes an expert at coaching from the sidelines while you do the talking for him. He's always shouting in your other ear, "Ask her this..." —or— "tell him that." And ladies, we all know how those three-way conversations grate on your nerves. After a half-hour of trying to carry on your conversation with his constant interruptions, you'd like to end them once and for all by adorning him with a choke collar fashioned out of the phone cord.

HUSBANDS WHO WORK AT HOME: THE KISS OF DEATH

The quickest way to insure that you will never again, not for even a nano-second, get to spend a moment alone for the rest of your natural life is to marry a man who works out of your home. You will have such unrealistic demands placed on your time that the thought of doing solitary in a high-security women's prison will start looking better every day. When you talk about the demands placed on a woman by the husband who is working at home, your job description shouldn't read HOUSEWIFE, it should read HOUSESLAVE. He will expect you to serve him gourmet breakfasts, lunches, and dinners with a smile. You won't even be able to seek refuge in the bathtub without him barging in to ask some inane question like what his mother's telephone number is. In recalling your marriage vows, forget the "for better" part — you're into the "for worse" part.

Strange but true, the man who works at home soon begins to look like his wife. And how can you have great sex with your mirror image? The only way to put the romance back into this marriage is to ship him off to the Betty Ford Clinic For Too Much Togetherness and let him detox for two months. When a man hasn't worn a suit in years and thinks that gamey undershirts and morning breath strong enough to kill small rodents are *de riguer* attire for his office at home, the "nooner" definitely loses its appeal.

THE "HELPFUL" HOMEMAKER

With the homebound hubby, there are two chances you'll ever get any housework done: SLIM and FORGET IT! One of his favorite pastimes is to follow you around with a white glove testing the tabletops for dust as you're cleaning and waxing them. Then he'll get down on all fours with a magnifying glass to inspect the carpet tracks made by the vacuum cleaner and "helpfully" point out the spots you've "missed." He will also become an expert at spotting a Windex streak on a pane of glass from 60 yards away. The cure is simple. The next time he follows you into the kitchen and explains that you aren't properly cleaning the accessory parts to the Cuisinart, remove the lid and ask him to take a closer look — then hit the switch. And if he still doesn't back off, as you're fixing his lunch, tell him a sandwich isn't the only thing you're going to *serve* him with.

Indeed, we love our husbands but PULEEZE — we need to have our space! When we get a day off from work, why do *they* have to take one off too? Is it just a subconscious need to aggravate us? More than one wife has been driven from her home, seeking refuge in the solace of her car, driving in aimless circles around a parking lot just for a breather. And then your worst nightmare comes true — when the car phone rings and you hear his sweet voice asking, "Hi, when are you coming home? I need you to rotate my shoe trees."

THE CLINGING VINE HUSBAND: HOW TO PERMANENTLY PRUNE HIS ROOTS

This is a well understood variation on the same theme. These guys are the ones who find it too painful to even go into the backyard and plant marigolds without an audience of one — you! It's hard to believe that this is the same man you didn't see for weeks at a time when you were dating. His strongest commitment in those days was, "I'll see you around." But marriage has a funny way of anatomically joining you at the hip. In self-defense, the beleaguered wife should read up on my sure-fire ways to LOSE HIM for an entire afternoon:

1. Suggest he accompany you to Loehmanns, where he will be forced, for the next four hours, to hold your purse and shopping bags while sitting with 60 snoring retired men who are all wearing pacemakers and have hair growing out of their ears.

2. Tell him it's important he go with you to your child's 5th grade annual Spelling Bee. Hype it by recounting how last year's 13 hour Bee featured two kids battling it out until midnight in a sudden death spell-off of the word pneumonoultramicroscopicsilicovolanoconiosis.

3. Say you need him to go wallpaper shopping with you at a new discount warehouse where they stock over 650,000 rolls from floor to ceiling. Explain that you value his input — plus

85

he'll have to climb the racks to get at the 95 rolls you'll be selecting together.

4. Send him to the grocery store with 50 expired coupons and a shopping list two legal pads long. Of course, he won't come home with one item even remotely resembling anything on your list. However, you will surely get another couple of hours respite as he is remanded into the custody of the assistant manager and grilled like a hot dog for trying to tender illegal coupons.

Be aware, the one problem with this tactic is he will come home with some unbelievable substitutions, leaving you to wonder if you wrote the list in English or Arabic:

a. You asked for a can of pimentos — he returns with a bushel of jalapeños.

b. You requested the personal hygiene product FDS — instead, he went to the florist and wired flowers FTD.

c. You requested the Family Size Tide — he ordered the Super-Duper-Economy Size (For The Republic of China) which is delivered to your door via semitrailer.

d. You wanted two pounds of hamburger — he cut a deal for a side of beef which could fill your puny freezer ten times over. So each family member will have to consume six Porterhouse steaks per meal over the next two weeks before the meat begins to sprout greenish-purple fuzz all over it.

e. You wrote down two packages of dust bags — he brings home two douchebags.

THE EXORCISE ROOM

One thing you must never do with the helpless husband is leave your home entrusted to his care for more than two hours at a time. If, for some reason, you have to be gone for a week, you will return to find your home now has the ambience of the Amityville Horror. As you approach the front door, you will immediately hear a voice from Hell shouting "GET OUT!" But on closer inspection, it turns out to be one of the guys from the Board of Health who is there to place a "CONDEMNED" sticker across your front door. If you dare to enter, this is what you'll find:

1. Your best designer towels, soiled beyond recognition and strewn all over the house starting from the bathroom and ending up in the kitchen. They will be submerged in a wake of powdery mildew, obliterating selective letters on the **St. Laurant** signature so it now beckons you with the fiendish greeting: S   L u   t.

2. A dishwasher with enough organic matter in it to grow Kudzu from seedlings in addition to the exotic Spanish Moss growing on the outside — all due to his innate inability to locate the "ON" button.

3. A carpet which has been organically fertilized with such an unprecedented amount of animal droppings, crushed cheese doodles, pizza crusts, and cigar butts, that it has spontaneously sprouted swamp grass.

4. The pets are suffering from severe dehydration, and the level of water in the aquarium has

dropped so low that the fish are swimming sideways.

5. Your terrified cleaning lady is bolting out the front door screaming and making the sign of the cross on her chest after taking in the unholy disaster inside.

6. So much grease on the countertops, house flies coming in for a landing skid and crash into the wall.

7. Due to a toilet left unflushed for a week, the gaseous atmosphere of the bathroom is the same composition as that found on the planet Venus.

8. When you open the refrigerator, you will see bacterial cultures which have had enough time to grow and mutate into a new screeching lifeform similar to the creature in "Aliens."

9. Your bed has become a repository of crumbs, Chinese takeout cartons, and half-eaten Hoagies. You could either cater a party for 12 from it or invite the roaches to dinner for a year.

10. Since the windows haven't been opened all week, the air is saturated with the bouquet of cigar smoke, bean dip, and farts. While women are normally exposed to these fumes in small doses on a regular basis, a week's concentration of this noxious combo will be more caustic to the lungs than mustard gas.

LAND OF THE LOST:
THE CLOSET THAT TIME FORGOT

Does this scenario sound familiar? You have busted your butt to get dressed, put on your makeup, and be ready to walk out the door at 8:00 o'clock sharp with your husband for his boss's dinner party. Now, at 7:59, in the upstairs bedroom, your husband is standing there staring off into space, butt-naked except for his garters, because he can't find anything he's supposed to be wearing that evening. He begins weeping uncontrollably because he knows that those old supernatural forces have once again conspired against him to mysteriously claim every garment he had planned on wearing. The explanation is simple. The helpless husband has once again fallen victim to the following paranormal phenomena:

1. Located right in the middle of his closet at 40 degrees latitude by 98 degrees longitude, by some freak of nature, the *Bermuda Triangle* has been duplicated. And every time he takes a shirt off the hanger to wear for the evening, it is sucked into another dimension before he can get it out of the closet. This leaves him in a state of total befuddlement as he shouts these familiar words to you: "Honey, where is that damned shirt? I just had it right here in my hand just two seconds ago and now it's gone!"

2. The second supernatural phenomenon takes place in his sock drawer where, for some inexplicable reason, a *Black Hole* has come into existence. And through it, one sock from each pair is sucked away beyond space and time,

never to be reunited again. Also, the *Black Hole* can operate selectively by choosing the color of socks he has intended to wear on any given occasion, luring them into an ominous place where even the USS Enterprise would not dare to go.

3. Cufflinks frequently fall prey to *poltergeist* activity. One minute they are in his hands — the next, they are jumping off his palm and playfully rolling under the bed and into an unreclaimable time warp.

4. Dress slacks become the focus of the supernatural process called *dematerialization*. They will vaporize into thin air right off their hangers. This is a frequent occurrence, always taking place just prior to a Saturday night on the town.

Up against these insurmountable odds, is it any wonder that the helpless husband needs all the assistance he can get? Unfortunately, it's the wife who is always enlisted as the *"ghostbuster"* and has to spend the next several hours trying to track down these items — often in futility.

So the husband does the best he can, and emerges from his room two hours late, dressed like a man who is color blind, night blind, and legally blind. You just as well to put a tin cup and pencils in his hand and let him attend the social function dressed in the truly unique outfit he managed to scrape together from the laundry hamper. But brace yourself. He will be making his grand entrance wearing a rumpled blue seersucker summer suit which the dog has used for a bed all week, a red plaid flannel shirt, one green/one black socks, one cufflink, and an inside-out undershirt which looks like it got up and walked over to him by itself.

And if his things keep disappearing at this astounding rate, it's only a matter of time until you open the refrigerator one morning only to find *his* picture on the milk carton.

SECTION B:
THE DO-IT-YOURSELF HUSBAND

CONTRACTING FOR CATASTROPHE

There are husbands out there who truly believe that there is NOTHING in the house they cannot fix themselves. The owner of every Time-Life How To book since time began, this husband's reputation for being able to fix anything is legend — in his own mind, of course.

Naturally, Bob Vila is his idol, and he has purchased every video Bob has ever made including his latest — an autobiography called,
Bob Vila's Hardware Story:
A Man and His Nuts.

Whenever a maintenance problem arises in the house, like a terminal disease, the family tries to hide it from him as long as possible. Because once he finds out, he's a man with a mission — to seek out and destroy all that is left standing. He'll disappear into his workroom, a mild-mannered three-piece-suited guy, and emerge seconds later in his new persona: *Mr. Mega-Handyman* wearing his suspendered coveralls and a leather tool belt strapped to his waist and fully loaded, brandishing every latest power tool on the market. Scary sight! This guy would rather cause mass destruction than pay one red cent to any repairman in the country.

Once he's let loose, there's no telling how many thousands of dollars you'll end up owing to repair the devastation he'll inflict when a simple $29.95 service call would have been all it cost you. These are some of the jobs he's going to tackle:

PLUMBING

Make sure your flood insurance is paid up. When changing the washer on the bathroom sink, he will always forget to shut off the main water valve. You'll need to rent Noah's Ark to keep your kids and pets safely afloat until all the water subsides — or can be sucked into a Wet-Vac over the period of 40 days and 40 nights.

HEATING

The do-it-yourself husband will say it's a snap to replace the copper pipe on your gas furnace. He will handily extract his giant lug wrench from his tool belt and try to remove those lug nuts that have been corroding on the furnace for the last 20 years. After trying to loosen them for hours unsuccessfully, in frustration he'll begin beating them to death with the handle. Carelessly connecting the new hose, he will have no idea that he did it backwards — and neither will you, until the family wakes up the next morning with headaches that feel like you've been inhaling a houseful of radon all night.

Then you will be forced to flee your home and take up residence at the Embassy Suites for a mere $159 per night — weekend rates slightly higher. The whole thing will end up costing you approximately the same as the downpayment on a new Lexus.

REFINISHING FLOORS

This process will ultimately become a textbook lesson in the TIME-LIFE How To Toxify Yourself

With Household Chemicals series. Because he is penny wise and pound foolish, your handy dandy man will not buy the mask and goggles necessary to protect his eyes and lungs from the dust. And the minute he begins to use his new 50 hp $600 industrial power sander, he'll look like he is standing in the middle of a Sahara Desert sand storm. We're talking zero visibility. In addition, the dust will coat his lungs so fast he'll turn blue and pass out before he finishes the first square foot of floor. However, this will only sideline him temporarily. After the paramedics revive him with an oxygen mask and a stiff intramuscular injection of adrenaline, he'll be ready to have another go at it. Two weeks later, the floors will be sanded but the entire contents of your home will be covered with a layer of sawdust six inches thick. And each time you vacuum it off, more will mysteriously appear in its place from out of nowhere. This stuff will materialize year after year, just like those Christmas tree pine needles do in your carpet.

The next near-lethal exposure will come from the varnish he's using to stain the floors. Forsaking the rubber gloves which run into a costly $1.98 per dozen, his skin will absorb this product producing symptoms of dizziness, nausea, and disorientation. However, because he normally feels like this on a good day — he'll ignore it and keep working.

The parting shot comes with the application of the polyurethane coating to the finished floor. Always in a rush to get the job done, your handy hubby will apply three coats in succession, allowing for no drying time in between applications. Not only this, but he will do it on a rainy day when the humidity is around 100%, eliminating any chance that this surface will ever dry completely before your 30-year mortgage is paid off.

BUILDING A CARPORT

God forbid. But it happens to the best of homes. He faithfully watched Bob Vila build one in six easy lessons, but if he finishes yours in six years it will be a miracle. The problem here is that he will want to make vital additions to the basic structure — like a john, a wet bar, and a library to house all those "How-To" books he's collected since 1949. But, you know what? This extra room isn't such a bad idea, because at the end of the six years, he'll have a nice place to move into after the divorce.

So ladies, that's the picture of the men who work IN the home and ON the home. Even though they are very different personalities, they spend their entire lives working diligently towards the same goal: the total destruction of your home and your sanity.

QUIZ V

1. The helpless husband needs an instruction manual to:
   a. make toast
   b. dress himself
   c. turn on a light
   d. have sex

   * d — *with you, or by himself*

2. Once the retired husband has been around the house for six months, you will need to:
   a. seek psychiatric help
   b. find him another job (and preferably in another city!)
   c. hire a hit man
   d. *hit* him yourself

   * b — *but change it to "preferably on another continent!"*

3. You are sick in bed. The helpless husband is forced to make dinner for himself. He will:
   a. burn down the kitchen trying to light the *electric* stove
   b. try to toast marshmallows by placing them directly on a burner
   c. cause a nuclear meltdown by putting the cast iron skillet in the microwave
   d. fight Cujo for the Kibbles N' Bits

   * *definitely a and c — so keep your holocaust policy updated*

4. Caution: The helpless husband could lose the tip of a finger:
   a. operating the Cuisinart
   b. grating carrots
   c. chopping onions
   d. inserting his Preparation H

   * d — *it's possible he could lose his arm, too*

5. You ask your helpless husband to run the school carpool. To insure that he accomplishes this task successfully, he'll need:
   a. at least a month of driving lessons beforehand
   b. photo IDs of the children
   c. you to "talk him through it" on the car phone
   d. a Trip-Tik from the AAA to locate the school

   * *none of the above* — *to insure success, you'll have to do it yourself*

CHAPTER 6

MACHO MEETS MARSHMALLOW:

The Health Nut
vs.
The Couch Potato Husband

SECTION A:
THE HEALTH NUT HUSBAND

The first thing you're going to need to do in order to co-exist with a health nut husband is to get your buns to the gym and learn to bench press 350 pounds of iron. And this is merely to get your biceps pumped up enough to be able to hoist the 500 pounds of supplies per week you'll be carrying out of the health food store for him. If you've ever noticed, health foods are always packaged and sold by the *barrel,* not by the pound. The only small quantity of any food substance you can buy in one of these places is Shitakke Mushrooms. But they go for about $6000 an unsavory ounce, so chances are you won't have to worry about them, anyway.

THE HUNT FOR RED GARBANZOS

You'll have to become proficient at finding those out-of-the-way health food stores. First of all, these places are always located well off the beaten path — like in the alfalfa fields of Oregon or on old dried-up communes in Taos. Run by burned-out Charles Manson look-alike hippies, the whole place is stuck in a time warp from the 60's. The feeling of deja-vu is overwhelming when you get a load of the men and women, scooping their raw oats from a barrel, clad in bell bottoms, love beads, and shoulder length hair so greasy it looks like wet strands of pasta.

First timers beware: immediately upon opening the door, you will be assaulted by a mixture of smells from zillions of vitamin capsules, sprouts, wheat germ, and barrels of dried seaweed permeating the adobe walls which have been fortified by Buffalo Chips. You'll be thinking, "Boy, I must be getting healthier by the minute just inhaling this stuff." Not ten seconds later, you'll run out of the store and promptly blow lunch all over the dirt sidewalk.

Clear out your cupboards, ladies. Once your man gets on this health-kick bandwagon, you'll be importing bales of hay for his breakfast. Here are a few rules you're going to have to follow to keep a "Health Food Kitchen," (which is quite similar in principle to keeping a Kosher Kitchen without having to bother with the Milchig and Fleishig* thing):

1.   HERB TEA.

Deep six your precious coffee pot forever. He will only allow you to serve that foul-smelling loose tea sold by the bushel, because all Self-Appointed Nutritionists who are diplomates of the Third Grade will tell you that coffee causes brain damage, cataracts, and blocked sperm tubes. And we all know how messy the first two can be.

2.   KELP.

It's a well-known fact that Educated Aquatic Animals everywhere have totally rejected this plant form as food because of:

   a. its exceedingly obnoxious flavor

---

* Correct spelling supplied to Shiksa author via Uncle Marvin in Orlando, Florida.

b. its tendency to make them produce those embarrassing telltale gas bubbles that float to the top of the water.

But the health nut will insist it's pleasing to the palate and you should at least give it a try. However, this advice is coming from a man who will spend the next four hours retching — commencing immediately after he ingests the first spoonful. But before we write off this foodstuff as totally unpleasant to the palate, a fact should be noted. Nine out of ten doctors agree that, in their medical judgement, anyone who eats Kelp has been born without taste buds.

3. PROTEIN POWDER.

This is bought by the 80 gallon drum which lasts a week or two at most. It is tossed into the blender with raw eggs and lowfat milk to produce a satisfying high-energy breakfast drink. There is only one minor side effect in that while the person is drinking it, he is simultaneously forming gallstones the size of bowling balls.

4. PINTO, LENTIL and GARBANZO BEANS.

Said to be high in vitamins, minerals, and methane gas, these little devils will be responsible for creating human "wind" currents approaching gale force. You should be cautioned to batten down all glass windows, nail all furniture to the floor, and remove pets and other life forms well downwind of your husband as he passes through the room after eating them.

5. BRAN MUFFINS, BRAN CEREAL, and BRAN POTATOES.

Ultimately, the health nut will become hopelessly obsessed with the state of his bowels. Fearing that his colon is not receiving enough roughage (i.e., the daily equivalent of ingesting six balls of raw twine), he will attempt to get the M.D.R. by speed-balling bran and oats directly into his lower bowel. It's one thing to be regular, another to be unstoppable. Most colon-obsessives won't be satisfied they're getting enough fiber until they get up off the john and find a bale of hay sticking out of the bowl.

6.   SUSHI.

Unless you're into chewing on raw bait and amenable to nine different fish parasites sharing your intestine, I'd let him fight the Yuppies for counterspace at the Sushi Bar by himself.

7.   TOFU.

This revolting bean curd foodstuff is the mainstay of the health nut's diet. And you will have to learn how to cook approximately 2,388 different tantalizing dishes with it including the wildly popular "tofu aspic" and "carp with tofu stuffing." We're talking real crowd-pleasers here — providing that the crowd has recently had all their taste buds singed off. Many are in agreement that tofu makes a strong health conscious statement. Like, "Eat this and then you die." And because of its high perishability, you will have to buy tofu daily. However, if you do run out, simply substitute something more nutritious and equally palatable: spackling compound.

8.   VITAMINS A-Z.

You will need to add on a separate pantry to hold all his bottles of these "essential" vitamins, most trace minerals found on this planet and some from Jupiter, amino acid tablets, garlic, bee pollen, ant hormones, powdered toad warts, and Oil of Olay. The average cost of these items will run about

$90.00 per week. And since the human body only retains the nutrients it can actually use, in the course of a normal day, he will pee out about $89.95 worth.

9. SPROUTS.

They must be harvested daily, preferably from a site irrigated with fresh running water — like the Love Canal. The health nut will add them to his salads, his cereal, and his tofu-burgers. High in nitrogen and fiber, the sprouts remain for an average of about three months in the lower intestine before they can be broken down into an undigestible mass small enough to be eliminated but just large enough to clog up your toilets. They also make great stuffing for throw pillows.

10. BROWN RICE.

This too will become a major staple of his diet. It must be grown in organic rice paddies, tended exclusively by starving Asians who are paid 30 cents a year for working 18 hour days in the fields while wearing unwieldy straw hats. The fields must be fertilized with only the purest of raw human sewage, aged with the help of yeast tablets,and carefully dumped over each unhusked kernel, thus giving it its characteristic rich brown color.

THE GYM: PERFECTING HIS PUMPTITUDE

Be prepared for your health nut to spend an average of 168 hours per week tending to his body at a bona fide health club. There he will find enough specialized training programs plus enough wall-to-wall mirrors to keep him engrossed with his biceps and gluteals from morning to midnight. He will become fanatical about many of the programs the club has to offer like:

1. CIRCUIT WEIGHT TRAINING.

This is where large machines bearing the capability of crushing your bones to powder are positioned in a circle around the room. Hence, the term "circuit." Set up in theory like an electrical light conduit, those overblown weight training spotters are the only dim bulbs found in the circuit. These are guys who have trouble forming complete sentences and move their lips when they read (those who *can* read, that is). They have spent years pumping up their bodies to such huge proportions that they can not do even the simplest tasks: like scratching their fannies.

Anyway, your beloved will strain, huff, and puff, attempting to lift huge amounts of weight with his various body appendages. The spotter does have a very important function, however. He is there to watch the great hooters on all the women wearing spandex training bras. His other job is to occasionally inform your husband, while he is bench-pressing 500 pounds, that the veins in his temples are within seconds of rupturing. And after executing his 506th squat thrust, the spotter has an obligation to inform your husband that he is building up one of the world's most overdeveloped hernias.

2. THE STAIRMASTER.

This is the latest word in cardiovascular workouts. However, most people don't know that it isn't new at all. It's actually an instrument of torture originally patented and used by the Viet Cong. What it entails is simply walking up the equivalent of 50,000 stairs pitched at a 90 degree angle at an escalating pace. Degree of difficulty is measured by how many vital organs you rupture per 20 steps.

3. THE TANNING BOOTH.

If men were to tell the truth, this is the main reason why they go to these dumb clubs in the first place. After all that hard work building up their pecs, abs, and penile implants, they want to show them off to their best advantage. This is best accomplished by sporting a healthful-looking ultra-violet light induced tan which turns the skin to the same color as a kumquat. And to highlight their tanned pecs, they will never appear semi-nude again without adding gobs of that "appetizing" body oil which not only adds definition to their budding muscles but gives them Wessonality as well. Feeling pumped and sexy, your well-oiled husband will come home and immediately want to make love. But take caution not to jump on him until he's showered off, or you'll slide across his body and hit the headboard at 55 mph.

4. THE STEAM ROOM.

Possibly some of the most unattractive sights known to the human race will be congregated in this one small space. Unlike Chippendales' you wouldn't pay a cover charge to see what's on exhibition here. On "exhibition" are flabby butts, butts with enough hair on them to comb into a pompadour, butt cheeks with cracks so wide they could catch a basketball between them, and butts so underdeveloped they can't even keep a towel up. On second thought, women would happily pay a cover charge — if these guys would cover up!

5. THE COMMUNAL JACUZZI.

Touted as "good for your health," in reality this is one place where you can find more scum floating on top of the water than in a stagnant bog. Talk about your breeding ground for bacteria! Even the germs take penicillin before getting into that water. But men love to sit in there, ostensibly to relax their overworked muscles. However, women are smart enough to know that the only reason a man would endure sitting in such a fulminating bacterial colony is to get a closer view of all the women's boobs bobbing and floating on the water gushing out of the jacuzzi jets. So be aware that this environment will not be able to relax EVERY muscle in a man's body.

STRENUOUS VACATIONS

More bad news for wives of health fanatics. Health nuts will not rest until they make sure you are sharing every moment of strain and torture right along with them. You will never again be able to go to a beach and relax on your butt reading trashy novels. You know — what a vacation should be all about. Instead, the health nut will have you engaged in activities that were only made for people in big need of electro-shock therapy.

Instead of touring the wine country on a bus and getting trashed as you were meant to do, you will now have to bicycle through the territory for six butt-blistering days on end. But the worst part of it is that he will make you wear those horrendous spandex bicycle pants with the foam rubber crotch. So you will look like a monkey in heat, sporting these huge vaginal lips and wearing a stupid-looking bicycle helmet on your head. Large numbers of people will gather to watch you ride by, exclaiming in a collective group these words of encouragement, "Gee, you two look like a couple of dorks."

Another trip straight out of hell is when the health nut asks you to exchange your weekend of shopping and Broadway plays in New York City for an entry into the New York Marathon. He will have you both training for six months, running for miles along sandy beaches littered with hazardous medical supplies. When your calf muscles collectively show an increase of $^1/_{16}$", he'll tell the entire family you are both entering in top form. Then you will suffer the ultimate humiliation when you are both shown on the 6 o'clock news crawling across the finish line dead last, wearing oxygen masks and soiling yourselves from terminal diarrhea.

One of life's worst moments will be when the health nut husband asks you to join him white water rafting in some remote location south of the Mason-Dixon Line. Here you will be accosted by certain indigenous dangers intent upon sharing your raft such as poisonous water snakes, man eating mosquitos, and the three backwoods guys from "Deliverance." At some point early on in this vacation, you will actually have a "death experience" (note: this is not the same as a "near death" experience). This occurs when you fall off the raft, are swept downstream at 90 m.p.h., and knock your head against giant boulders in the river no less than 60 times on each square inch of exposed cranial surface. You will then sink to the bottom of the river and actually *choose* to stay there and drown, rather than come up and have to get back into the raft and listen to Bubba and his buddies suggestively saying to your husband: "You got some mighty pretty lips on you, Boy."

SECTION B:
THE COUCH POTATO HUSBAND

The antithesis of the health nut is the passive Couch Potato husband; the ultimate spectator in life from his Laz-E-Boy recliner. This man actually possesses a Master's Degree from Princeton, but after years of non-stop cable TV watching, he has effectively lowered his I.Q. to that of a spud.

He's not anything like the health nut who agonizes over whether he's getting his minimum daily requirements of vitamins and minerals. Quite the contrary, he's happiest when he's getting the maximum daily requirement of The Couch Potato's Version of the Four Basic Food Groups:

   a. Doritos
   b. Coors
   c. Slim Jims
   d. Pork Rinds

These cardio-vascular treats have both good and bad points. The bad news is that they will put even more plaque in his major arteries than they will on his teeth. But the good news is when enough of them collect under all the cushions in back of the couch, he could actually open a 7-11 Franchise from where he sits.

This husband has become a permanent fixture in the room — and exactly like the furniture, he must be dusted daily to remove the cobwebs, waxed, and vacuumed around ("Once again, would you please lift your feet up"). Plus he requires an annual steam cleaning to suck the volcanic cigar ashes out of his pores. The Couch Potato is the rare exception in the human race who will actually welcome the opportunity of having a salesman from the Linkletter Lounge Chair and Fleece Company come into his home. And after the five-hour sales pitch, the salesman will execute the custom "in-house butt cast," making the exact fit required to comfortably accommodate his expansive behind. All this for a mere $1200 down (the drain) and $79.99 per month for as long as his butt shall survive.

Housewives beware: prolonged immobility can cause the rapid loss of muscle tone in a couch potato, causing him to roll off the couch. But you'll know this has happened by the familiar mournful cry: "Help, I've fallen and I can't get up!"

If you're too busy, just ignore his cries. Eventually the kids will get tired of tripping over him and haul his sorry butt back onto the couch.

Once comfortably ensconced on his couch again, he will NEVER move. This is going to drive the Couch Potato's wife bananas. She'll attempt to fight back in her own way by doing little annoying things like making hospital corners out of his pants legs. But nothing short of a power failure or a full bedpan will move this guy unless the determined wife takes drastic measures and pulls out all the Big Guns:

1. Discreetly place your kid's Red Ant Farm directly under the cushions, leaving the trap door open. These are the kinds of ants who squirt out their stinging formic acid by the quarts just

for fun. And for added excitement, make sure the ants haven't been fed for a week.

2. After an entire afternoon of back-to-back horror movies combined with too many brewskis, his head will start spinning around in 360 degree turns. Phone your local dioceses and enlist the aid of a priest to exorcise him out the damn front door.

3. Welcome all encyclopedia, insurance, magazine, and vacuum cleaner salesmen, and/or religious zealot recruiters (especially Jehovah Witnesses) warmly into your home. Direct them straight to the couch where he's vegetating and advise them of your husband's eagerness to hear every word of their sales pitch.

4. Install a gas-driven treadmill for his buns.

5. When his case of beer has taken its toll and placed his bladder in imminent danger of exploding, rush to all the bathrooms in your house just before the commercials and lock the doors.

6. Place your two-year-old's potty chair directly downwind of his Barcalounger.

7. Hot wire his channel changer.

    Cruel and unusual punishment? We think not. Those remote controls can take a lot of heat.

*   *   *

It could be a tough decision making up your mind between these two kinds of passive or aggressive personalities. No woman likes a man who is too macho or too wimpy. Maybe the best idea would be to go for a man who combines both traits: a passive-aggressive type. Then you will get a man who gets a thrill out of picking a fight with you, but is too much of a *wuss* to actually carry it out. This way you always win!

QUIZ VI

1. The couch potato husband exercises daily by:
   a. watching his Raymond Burr workout video
   b. occasionally readjusting his catheter bag
   c. doing beer can curls
   d. lifting his legs while you vacuum under them

   * d — *with the aid of his motorized E-Z Chair*

2. The couch potato shops for his Barcalounger at:
   a. Buns R Us
   b. Tub O' Fat Furniture
   c. Phil Rizzuto's Family Convalescent Store
   d. The Big and *Wide* Store

   * c — *Phil also lends you money at the "Family's" interest rate of 35% per day (the compounded fracture rate)*

3. The wife of a health nut husband can seek a divorce on the grounds of having to:
   a. brew cruel and unusual herbal teas
   b. attend cruel and punishing exercise classes
   c. be subjected to cruel and excessive gas emission
   d. prepare cruel and unpalatable Tofu dishes

   * c — *can also make you go deaf*

4. The vegetarian husband who runs 10 miles a day can easily be spotted in a crowd by:
   a. his sunken cheeks (both sets)
   b. the oxygen tanks strapped to his back
   c. looking for a skeleton in sneakers
   d. his becoming airborne in a 5 m.p.h. wind

   * a — *sometimes seen with a shriveled zucchini, too*

5. The Men's Steam Room at the health club is also known as:
   a. Wide-Ass Avenue
   b. Canyon View
   c. Butt Butte
   d. The Crackhouse

   * *you decide — whichever cracks you up*

CHAPTER 7

THE GOOD, THE BAD, AND THE UGLY:

The Sexual Athlete
vs.
The Party Animal
vs.
The Sexually Unathletic Husband From Hell

SECTION A:
THE PARTY ANIMAL HUSBAND

Hey, we wives have nothing against our husbands throwing a good party — except when we're the only ones in the family who don't get an invitation. In fact, if it wasn't for Tupperware, we'd never be invited to any parties at all. Unfortunately, this seems to be the rule rather than the exception when you marry a Party Animal. This kind of husband is a guy who basically, not only loves a party but never wants it to end. When the guests are dragging their weary bodies out of your house at 4 a.m., he's standing there hurt to the quick saying, "Was it something I said?"

He'll go to any lengths just to keep the party going for a few more minutes. When he reluctantly escorts the guests out the door, he'll beg them to stay for a couple of minutes longer in the driveway just to "watch the moon" with him — then he surprises the crowd by dropping his pants. And the buffoon considers this to be sophisticated humor!

One of his favorite pastimes is to regularly drop by his favorite bar for a couple of drinks with the boys on a Friday night — which wouldn't be so bad, except he ends up staying there until Monday afternoon. Unless the wife has the same IQ as a head of cabbage, she'll catch on to his old tricks after hearing the same old lame excuses year after year:

1.   THE HALF-TRUTH EXCUSE

"Honey, I'm just stopping off for ONE drink." What he fails to tell you is that he's drinking it from a five gallon martini glass.

119

2. THE "IT'S OUT OF MY CONTROL" EXCUSE

"Hello, honey, I'm calling from the car phone to tell you I'm on my way home, but I'm caught in a horrible traffic jam. It might be hours before I get home." Funny how this particular traffic jam occurs every Friday evening at 6 p.m. like clockwork and lasts about the same amount of time as it would take to drink 10 beers, smoke 20 cigarettes, and tell 30 dirty jokes.

3. THE MARTYR EXCUSE

"Honey, I really don't want to stay for this office party, but my friend Larry is uncomfortable going alone and *begged* me to go with him, and I just can't let him down." Now, Larry is a great looking, personable guy, who scores more babes in one night than the whole office does in a year. Like he really needs your husband, the man who's famous opening line to pick up women used to be, "Just do what I say and you won't get hurt." Right!

4. THE "YOU'D HAVE TO BE A *FLATLINER* TO BELIEVE THIS EXCUSE" EXCUSE

Honey, I know this is going to sound weird — but TRUST me. I was run off the road by three Biker Babes who poured liquor down my throat, took my pants off, trashed my car with an ax, and then took off and left me for dead. Can you come and get me?" So what do you do? Oblige him by sending him the *real* thing — a gal named "Slasher" from "Hell's Belles" to go pick him up and bring him home (after she works him over, for *real* of course.)

But women know all too well that there are times you'd be doing yourself a big favor by allowing him to party alone. Because when he's really in his cups, he will decide that it's time he revealed his hidden talents or things he thinks he is absolutely THE GREATEST on Earth at doing:

1. Dancing.

This is a man whose feet never touch a dance floor until he gets about five straight bourbons under his belt. And then, he suddenly thinks he's Patrick Swayze and should be giving dance lessons to Michael Jackson and M.C. Hammer.

He'll drag you out on the dance floor against your will and begin executing some "Dirty Dancing" moves of his own which are so obscene, they would have closed down production on the movie set. By this time, his arms and legs are operating independently of each other, yours, and the rest of his body — and he's got less rhythm than the Catholic Church. So he's not only making a total spectacle of himself, he's also making a total fool of himself. You are ready to go back to your table and crawl under it when he starts doing the Lambada solo out there. This sight is so humiliating that you would do anything to disavow any relationship with him, even if it meant enrolling yourself in the Witness Protection Program.

2. Making Love.

Why is it that when a man gets a few too many drinks in him, he automatically assumes the favorite of all his multiple personalities, the Rob Lowe Persona. Now he's ready for action. And let's face it, in his inebriated condition, his body has about the same degree of coordination as Joe Cocker's — if not worse. While his mind is conjuring up great sexual scenarios, his body is having serious problems responding because the millions of nerve endings in his vital organs have been thoroughly anesthetized. He'll give you a slobbering speech about "sailing with him on a sea of love," but he's completely unable to hoist the mainsail and his dinghy sinks.

He'll promise you a night you'll NEVER forget but what you get is a night you'd give ANYTHING to forget. You're in deep trouble. You realize that you're going to be held captive for at least an hour and a half of spastic foreplay followed by a three-hour marathon in which he miserably fails to consummate the session. All the while he is drooling in your ear about the "big things that are going to happen." A true anti-climactic statement if there ever was one. The only "big thing" that happens is when his 250 pound body passes out on top of you.

3. Driving.

When his blood alcohol level reaches .50, his macho-ego decides that only *he* is capable of driving, so he gets behind the wheel to drive the two of you home. In between the memory lapses he suffers on the road, he'll keep telling you he is Danny Sullivan (you should only be so lucky) — which isn't a total lie, because at that point, he really *can't* remember what his own name is. Naturally, after doing 96 mph for 10 minutes on a hairpin road, a cop will pull him over when you start grazing the guardrail on a narrow bridge.

Next, he decides to endear himself to the cop by saying, "Hey, good buddy, how the hell are ya?" — then tries to shake his hand. His contention of having "one drink" will look pretty lame after the balloon he blows up immediately disintegrates on contact from his toxic breath. Then he'll be asked to walk a straight line, which is a joke because how can he *walk* a line he can't even *see?* So he will amuse the crowd which has now gathered (of course, most are people who know you) by doing the "moonwalk" backwards 12 feet from the line. As the cop gets more and more irate, he will wreak the ultimate revenge by asking your inebriated husband to walk another straight line — this time on the railing above the bridge.

If he doesn't fall off, YOU will be issued the DWI, which in this case stands for "Driving With an Idiot."

SECTION B:
THE SEXUAL ATHLETE HUSBAND

THE OVERSEXED HUSBAND: A CASE STUDY OF DARREN B. (not his real name)

Here is a man who prides himself on his past conquests, advertising them proudly by wearing a belt with large conspicuous notches cut in it. He has been around so much, you will run across bumper stickers that say "Honk if you've had Darren." The man has had so many blind dates in his day, he should have won a free seeing-eye dog. But in retrospect, he did end up with a lot of dogs.

The most irritating thing about him is that he never fails to introduce references to his past love life into the conversation at any given moment. Here's a typical case:

"Would you like whipped cream on your pie, dear?"

"Ah, yes, whipped cream. That reminds me of the time I was in a motel room in Peoria with this girl, Kinki, and she showed me how to *top things off* with a can of Reddi-Whip...."

Can you believe this bogus guy? He obviously doesn't know that past sexual partners have the ability to cause dangerous diseases in present partners up to 10 years after the act. So in effect, you'll be sharing Kinki plus her past lovers' menagerie of antibiotic resistant viral strains — not to mention the organisms that were cultured in the whipped cream as well. Adding this to the numerous other women he's had in the past, we are talking about more partners than in a class action suit. And this situation will certainly not allow Darren to win his *case* with you — rather, you'll be *on* his case for the rest of his life.

DANGEROUS LIAISONS

The sexual athlete husband is a guy who loves to live on the edge. He's into doing it in unusual places which involve an element of danger or risk taking to heighten the excitement. But the wife of this man can hardly rise to a level of passion beyond "stone cold" when he opts for places like:

1. In the front seat of the car (while he's driving).
2. In front of a roaring fire (at a downtown warehouse).
3. Under the table at a posh restaurant in Washington, D.C., where you'll have to push Teddy aside to make room for yourselves.
4. Phone sex (in a booth).
5. While listening to a sensual rendition of Ravel's "Bolero" (from your front row orchestra seats).
6. On a Boeing 747 (during an emergency landing while you're both in the crash position).

THE NATURAL MAN

Even though the sexual athlete husband likes to do it with the frequency of lab mice, these men are against any form of birth control that interferes with *their* pleasure. They especially hate condoms. And naturally, this position (or any of the other 230 in their repertoire) is not in your best interest. They will complain bitterly saying, "Look, honey, I hate doing it with those things on. I just don't *feel* anything."

So tell him that makes two of you, and that should shut him up.

Sexual athletes are heavy into visual stimulation. Being connoisseurs of sexy negligees, they can't wait for the next issue of Playboy to see what lingerie the Bunny of the Month is barely wearing. So he'll ask you to dress provocatively for him and assume the same poses as the girls in a "Big 10" pictorial. But what wife wants to take a shower in shoulder pads and a football helmet? Also, those leather bras and stud-covered garter belts can inflict some nasty wounds when you're trying to execute a backbend over a boudoir chair with your legs spread so far apart they feel like they're in different time zones. Ouch!

Many sexual athletes really get hooked on those graphic poses contained in the "scratch n' sniff" centerfolds of Hustler. But the wife has to draw the line somewhere. She should set some ground rules with her husband about just how far she'll go. And exposing any part of her anatomy that only her gynecologist ever reaches is strictly off limits.

These guys are into marital aids in a big way. Every week they stop by Wanda's Whip Emporium to see what's new in the inventory. They love to come home and surprise you with a new present every week — wrapped in brown paper, and tied with a leather bow, of course. Here are some nifty items he'll choose for your "mutual" enjoyment:

1.   The "Raging Bull Vibrator."

This one has a circumference approximating a Goodyear tire and batteries powerful enough to jump start a diesel truck. It takes a 220 volt outlet to handle it, has forward and reverse gears, and can reach 6,000 r.p.m.'s in 20 seconds. This kind of power surge will send you into orbit so often you'll be able to qualify for frequent flier coupons.

2. The "French Tickler."

When you open up the package and get a load of those feathers, you'll reap the immediate benefits — you'll be laughing for days.

3. "Helen's Hot Love Oil."

Discovered as a crude petroleum product collected from Prince's leaking hair, this stuff gets hotter than Wok oil when you lick it. Actually, it tastes something like Wok oil, or maybe that's Yak oil — these technical things are so hard to remember. Anyway, when used selectively on the organ of your choice, utmost caution should be taken so you don't end up in the Emergency Room being treated for the World's Most Embarrassing Burn. (The only person you could possibly explain it to would be a "head nurse.")

4. "Chinese Love Balls."

Because of their alleged addictive powers, they are the main reason China is still an underdeveloped country today. The instructions are written in Chinese characters, and even though you can't read what they're saying — there's *no doubt* about what they're *doing!* You won't need Roget's Raunch Thesaurus to interpret them. But in all probability, unless you're hopelessly trashed on Sake, you won't ever get up the nerve or flexibility to follow what the picture is showing you to do.

5. Candy Pants.

If he won't eat your cooking, why would he try to eat these?

WARNING: One thing you NEVER want to do, ladies, is tell your husband anything about your past sex life no matter how innocent you think it is. There is a double standard operating here with the sexual athlete, and their minds automatically link you to the kinds of things they did in their heyday. And once you tell them anything about an old boy-friend or, God forbid, a one-night stand, they will never fail to dredge up those old indiscretions, and embellish them to the point where you would think you cruised dark alleys in fishnet stockings and a bunny stole for half your life before meeting him. And NEVER MENTION NAMES. Once he knows the name of a former lover, he'll track him down and accuse the two of you of still carrying on — even if the guy is now a grandfather, has no teeth, and is covered with warts.

SECTION C: THE SEXUALLY UNATHLETIC HUSBAND

Here is a man with so little prior experience, his idea of protection is wearing safety goggles to bed. The poor guy is so straight he could be an honorary Osmond. We know Muslim women who have more sexual street smarts than him. Do you get the picture?

Basically, he got married because he didn't like sex and believed most women don't like it either. So this man poses a particular challenge. And it's usually the very aggressive, oversexed women who go for this man to take on the ultimate challenge of turning him onto sex and into their personal love slave. They will dress up in a Victoria's Secret get-up that has more accesses than a Los Angeles freeway, pour on the perfume, and do their little dance until they are so hot to trot their garters are melting. Then they will crawl across the sheets, seductively cooing and licking their lips. When they reach him, he has either passed out in abject fear or has fallen asleep.

The guy has more excuses to avoid sex than a pregnant woman. Like he has a headache from blowing up the love toys, or the leather straps are giving him wrist burns, or the whip is making him nervous. What a wimp!! Can't a girl have any fun?

So what do you do with a guy like this? Unfortunately, not much.

It sure would be great, ladies, if we could marry a man who was the perfect combination of the party animal and the sexual athlete husband. Especially one who would consent to not only wearing a "party hat" at the party but afterwards in the bedroom, too. Now that would make one perfectly safe man and obviously too much to hope for!

Unfortunately, in the case of the sexually unathletic husband, there's no way to re-start his dead batteries. My best advice would be to buy some fresh ones for yourself and take matters into your own hands.

QUIZ VII

1. What does the party animal husband and Spuds MacKenzie have in common:
   a. laps up beer from a bowl
   b. sniffs the female guests
   c. can dance on all fours
   d. urinates on the carpet

   * all of the above and in the same order

2. The oversexed bisexual male has twice as great a chance of getting:
   a. AIDS
   b. Herpes
   c. Infectious binucleosis
   d. a date on Saturday night

   * d — plus a, b, and c by Sunday morning

3. Which foodstuffs are most frequently eaten by the oversexed husband?
   a. raw oysters
   b. ginseng root
   c. lotus leaves
   d. whipped cream, cherries and chocolate syrup

   * d — but only when his wife is wearing them

4. The sexually unathletic husband can be helped by watching motivational tapes made by:
   a. Dr. Ruth
   b. Jimmy Swaggart
   c. Rob Lowe
   d. Gary Hart

   * b — all footage shot while kneeling

5. The sexually unathletic husband prefers to have sex:
   a. once a month
   b. once — on his wedding night
   c. with an inanimate object
   d. alone

   * d — *his wife prefers it this way, too*

CHAPTER 8

WHOSE BEEMER IS THIS ANYWAY?:

The Yuppie
vs.
The Nerd Husband

SECTION A: THE YUPPIE HUSBAND

The Yuppie husband works very hard at developing and maintaining his Yuppie image by carefully watching and taking notes on how to be pretentious from the whining characters seen each week on "thirtysomething." Michael Steadman is his idol, from his button down shirts to his Johnston and Murphy 12 pound shoes. And he'll have you working your buns off to get as close to the Hope persona as humanly possible. This includes making you wear those (gag!) shapeless ankle-length jumpers with black flats and those passé headbands pushing back the straight wash n' wear hair. You know — that kind of anemic graduate school look. You'll have to sit around and look serious a great deal of the time, having in-depth conversations on important topics like the merits of Montessori vs. public kindergarten or virgin olive oil vs. extra-virgin olive oil. All this while maintaining a look of great consternation through these yawners, when you'd rather be doing ANYTHING else, including baiting live worms on fishing hooks.

You will have to work very hard at making your house look like old money, incorporating the duck motif in every room, along with a lot of Chippendale pieces (and I don't mean the kind that dance, either). Also, to maintain that blueblood façade, you're going to have to convince your parents that they must be called Buffy and Biff even though their real names are Marge and Ralph.

This carefully studied image means everything to the Yuppie husband. And as a Yuppie wife, you are going to have to learn the very important factors to be followed in establishing and keeping a Yuppie household. Here are some musts:

YUPPIE PUPPIES

They must be purebred Labs or West Highland White Terriers *only*. He considers Collies or Cocker Spaniels to be so bourgeoisie that the sight of them will make a Yup instantly ralph all over his madras bermudas. The dogs must be given names like *Rugger* or *Atherton* which are taken directly from the servants Mater and Pater abused on a regular basis during his childhood. The dogs must be outfitted with bona fide L.L. Bean neckerchiefs tied carefully in a triangle, hanging jauntily around their necks. Preferably being owned in pairs, the dogs must only be transported in the family Range Rover. If you try to put them in a Yugo or Honda, the dogs will immediately urinate all over the naugahyde seats to show their disdain for such déclassé taste.

Saturday afternoons are spent having "quality family time" by engaging in a rousing game of lawn football with the dogs and kids, carefully copied down to the last detail from old Kennedy pictures taken at Hickory Hill. And once perfected, they will appear on each year's Christmas Photo card sent to everyone in the Universe in hopes of demonstrating how *your* upscale Yuppie family makes *their's* look like the Clampetts. One problem, however. Rugger and Atherton usually tarnish the image by being caught off-guard pooping in the background much like their namesakes used to do.

YUPPIE FOOD

Eating the "right" kinds of designer foods is very important to the care and well-being of the developing Yuppie. He could blow his whole image in one swift moment if spotted eating foods which are currently on the "Out" list of "GQ" magazine. Here's a list of some items a Yup pantry must be carefully stocked with at all times:

1.   Balsamic Vinegar

The stuff is on every Yup's "in" list. It is to be carefully poured on salads, used in cooking, and displayed in a very noticeable place in the kitchen at all times. The Yup palate can whiff out the pedestrian Heinz brand from 1,000 yards away so don't dare try this substitute. Balsamic vinegar is important for maintaining that slightly pinched look around the Yuppie mouth, giving him that smug demeanor of superiority while he glibly recites phrases such as "Oh, Gawd, Dinky. Did the Richards actually buy a Broyhill sofa for their living room?" Or "You can't really mean that Dave publicly admits he went to a state college!"

2.   Evian or Perriér Water

This is such an "in" brand that any other simply will not do. If one dares to buy another label like "Polish Springs," the blueblood will fear it's accidental ingestion could cause him to grow facial wens and give him an overwhelming urge to take up the accordion. It is also of the utmost importance that he carry a 6 oz. bottle around the racquet club with him at all times, taking frequent swigs while prominently displaying the label. He could care less that it seems like one of the biggest rip-offs known to mankind at $3.59 plus tax for a six-pack of water. And even the fact that chimpanzees have been known to fall down hysterically laughing at the price doesn't deter him.

3. Homemade Pasta

Yuppies are really big on the fresh pasta thing, insisting it be handmade on the premises, as well as the accompanying sauce. But it will ultimately cause the Yuppie Wife terminal frustration, because the $600 pasta machines clog up every five minutes and break down no less than 12 times during the whole eight-hour preparation process. Then after the meal is finally eaten at 3 a.m., she has to spend another four hours trying to get the hardened dough out of the 2,000 little holes in the blades with a toothpick. Most wives end up losing it altogether by 4 a.m. and shove the whole pasta machine in the trash compactor, set it on "HIGH," and crush it beyond recognition.

4. Pâté de Foie Gras

Served on Carr's water table crackers, the Yuppie party is doomed to certain failure without it. It also must be prepared in a Cuisinart (an Oster will contaminate it), and lumped in generous quantities that resemble a well-formed goose turd on a cracker. The food snobs will delight in spending the greater part of the evening pretending they love this delicacy, and boast how they eat it at least twice weekly themselves. Then after the party is over, they will go home and spend the rest of the night alternately barfing and having the runs in their respective "his" and "hers" toilets.

5.   Oyster Stuffing

Any self-respecting Thanksgiving Yuppie Turkey will immediately expel any stuffing containing such plebian items as cornbread or sausage from any one or all of its untrussed orifices. Oyster stuffing must be prepared using only fresh oysters flown in from Bar Harbor, Maine, and which possess the same look and consistency as well-aged lungers. Anything of a lesser quality will cause your husband to fly into a rage and savagely lash you with his regimented striped tie in front of the children.

6.   Espresso Machine

This is *de rigueur* for every Yuppie kitchen counter. Although it will actually be used less than your old fondue pots which have been wrapped in mothballs since 1972, it will bring joy to your heart knowing you have to polish it twice daily with Brasso until your arm gets numb and tingles. And if you ever do decide to use it, the coffee produced will contain so much caffeine, it will be capable of snapping you out of a coma.

7.   The Wine Rack

It is the ultimate Yuppie who prides himself on being an oenophile. And although this sounds like he has some perverted sex disorder (which may or may not be true), it actually means a wine expert. Always searching for ways to educate his sophisticated palate, the Yup will subscribe to fine wine publications such as "The Ripple Register" and "Touring the Wine Country: Boone's Farm Revisited." These are a must to keep out on the coffee table, never opened, and subsequently used as coasters. The oenophile will rehearse the following phrases until he is able to recite them fluently at dinner parties or fine restaurants while making a big flourish of sniffing the bouquet and sloshing the wine around in his glass:

"This claret is full-bodied but definitely pretentious" or "I find this pedestrian in its predictability but capricious in its affability."

He will go on and on, like some overinflated gas bag until the other dinner guests are forced to retaliate by belching directly into his face to make him shut up.

YUPPIEKIDS

Children of Yuppies do not realize that the *au pair* girl is not their Mommy until they reach the age of about eight years old. This can be quite traumatic for them, not only because they will have to get to know their real Moms, also the children have been raised to speak Spanish. Consequently, they'll have to learn English as a second language. However, the Yuppie parents will try to resolve this dilemma by spending the afternoon in "The Learning Lab" buying the confused child $4,000 worth of remedial toys.

Yuppie parents are totally wrapped up in the process of choosing the "right" school for their children. This is crucial to their social standing in the community — and once in a while the kids get a good education, too. They consider any school with the word "public" in its title to mean certain brain death for the kiddies. So the quest begins early on to enroll their kid in the best private school they can find. And if they *can* afford it, it's definitely the wrong one.

Here's a list of the types of schools which are a "must" for a self-respecting Yuppiekid to attend. Failure to do so could jeopardize their social standing to the point where they might be forced to play tennis on "public" (God forbid!) courts.

1. Pre-School

Any institution with the name "Country Day" anywhere in its name is acceptable. For example, "Happy Acres Reform and Country Day School" would pass muster with the Yups. The length of the school day is crucial. Yuppie Moms favor 8 a.m.-bedtime so they will have enough time to attend Junior League, Save the Whales, and How To Throw Pretentious Birthday Party meetings.

2. Private Elementary School

The private schools are so jammed up with applications from desperate Yuppie parents that the waiting lists are becoming impossible. To assure a place for their kids, more and more Yups are enrolling their kids while they're still fetuses. And in the advent of medical technology, we now find a situation where masses of women are barraging the school doors carrying vials revealing pink rings (confirming that conception has taken place) and demanding an application.

3. Preparatory Schools

This is the only way to go for the Yuppie teen-ager. The term preparatory school is derived from the Latin roots: *a. Preppus* — literally translated as "offspring of a snob" and *b. atory* — meaning "wearing khaki."

These are establishments that cost the same per year as the price of an average suburban home (not including books and building fund). The kids are strongly urged to board there, because a day commuter gives about as much prestige to the family as if he had enrolled in the American School of Diesel Training. But the right Prep school is an essential prerequisite for getting into a prestigious East Coast college. In fact, the Prep school education plus a $50,000 "donation" from the old man will just about assure the student of getting into any Ivy League college of his choice.

4.   The Ivy League College

There are only ten of these prestigious colleges, all located on the East Coast, because no one can get ivy to grow on adobe brick in California. Potential students are rigorously screened and must have mastered these prerequisites at their Prep Schools before being accepted:

  a. Must be able to chug four pitchers of beer in ten minutes standing on a small tabletop and remain upright without falling off, vomiting in his shoes, or passing out.

  b. Must possess a wardrobe comprised of no less than ten pair of khaki pants or skirts (or both in the more liberal colleges), six pair of madras bermudas, six pair of Docksiders, and several hundred shirts all bearing the bona fide Polo emblem. Any knockoff copies with bogus emblems purchased from street vendors can be spotted a mile away and will result in the immediate expulsion of the student.

c. A student must be able to afford the expense of traveling over Winter Break to Aspen where he will get drunk, ski the black slopes, and break both legs. Also acceptable is to drive to Fort Lauderdale in his Corvette, where he will get drunk, fall off a surf board, and give himself a major brain concussion. Any geek who opts to spend any time whatsoever during Break at his parents' home will be the object of intense ridicule and blackballed from the Greek system for the duration of college life.

d. A student must be tapped by at least one private society in the Ivy League school. Such prestigious societies at Yale University, for example, are Skull and Bones, Scroll and Key, and Surf N' Turf. Members are selected by secret ballot and inducted during a ritualistic formal ceremony involving candlelight, cap and gown, and sheep membranes.

THE YUPPIEMOBILE

Perhaps the most obnoxious aspect of this sub-culture is their strict adherence to the Yuppie Code of Automobiles. The code is so rigid, that it allows for no deviation. The choices are clear-cut:

a. BMW

Or nauseatingly referred to by all Yuppies as the *Beemer* — as in, "I can't seem to get my Beemer up today."

b. Volvo

Stamped with the American Yuppie Carpooling Seal of Approval, the Volvo is chosen because it makes an important statement about its owners: "I am not nouveau-riche like the people who drive gauche Cadillac Eldorados and wear obnoxious diamond pinkie rings."

c. Range Rover

This is the perfect second car for Yuppies to transport their kids and dogs to their summer homes. They have great roof racks which are ideal for "inconspicuously" carting skis, mountain bikes, and low-class relatives along for a free vacation.

All other models of cars are to be avoided as strenuously as Italian cut suits. This includes Ford Escorts, Nissan Sentras, Chevrolet Caprices, or anything referred to by the masses as a "pick-em-up truck." Accoutrements like private school decals are encouraged, as well as "Baby on Board" signs, soccer league bumper stickers, personalized license plates, car phones, and Perriér dispensers.

Certain objects so reek of middle class mentality that they are universally banned from Yuppie cars. These objects include:

   a. Garfield dolls with suction cups on their feet that stick to the windows

b. Redneck dolls on the dashboard that drop their pants and moon passing motorists

c. Religious statuary displayed anyplace in the car

d. Hula dolls or dogs with the wobbling neck seen through the rear window

e. Any kind of bumper sticker that contains the word "Jesus" in any context whatsoever

YARE YUPPIES

The *pièce de résistance* that represents your arrival into Yup society is when you purchase a sailboat. This is the ultimate way for the privileged to express that *noblesse oblige* attitude other than peering down his nose over his wire-rimmed Ivy League issue spectacles. And the first thing he'll want to do is give his boat a moniker like "The WASP" which leaves no doubt as to where he's coming from. It automatically separates him from the hoi polloi who sport muscle T-shirts and day-old chin stubble while buzzing around in those *déclassé* cigarette boats.

The huge problem associated with sailing, as any surviving wife will tell you, is that even the mildest mannered husband turns into Captain Queeg the minute you leave the dock. He will be SCREAMING orders at you, and have you running up and down the deck until you're in oxygen debt. In general, he'll make the entire family so crazed, they'll be kicking the rats out of the way to jump ship before them. This is such a frequent occurrence that you'll often find divorce lawyers out circling the waters with the other sharks, picking up $40,000 in retainers in a single afternoon.

The best part of the day is when the Yuppie hubbie docks his boat (after a 30 minute excursion) in their private slip five feet from the Old Guard and Right Guard Country Club. This is when he hoists the sail bearing the Chivas Crest, signaling the start of his favorite aspect of the boating experience — the extended Happy Hour. Besides, it's a perfect opportunity for him to show off his double-breasted Navy blazer, ascot, white ducks and Sperry Top-siders. After four hours of drinking tequila shooters, everyone is welcomed aboard (including the illegals from Colombia who passed them on the high seas with the Coast Guard riding shotgun on their tails). Not only will yachting stories be traded with Juan Valdez, but some primo ganga weed as well. By 4 a.m., the Yups are so faced, they have inadvertently promised their teenage daughters' hands in marriage to the sons of the Medellin Kingpins for half a kilo of Colombian Gold. By 8 a.m., after realizing what they've done, the flag is lowered to half-mast.

All in all, it's not a bad deal to marry into a socially conscious Yup family. But it's not easy to be accepted without the proper social credentials. You will have to convince them that you come from good stock, which means producing a pedigree — and proof that all of your shots are up to date. You can clinch the deal when you show them your Family Crest — and don't forget your toothbrush.

* * *

But if all this social hoopla is not your cup of Earl Grey tea, you might consider marrying the type of man who has *no* social standing — the nerd. These guys are so out-of-it when it comes to social class, the only "Blue Book" they've heard of is the one where you look up car prices.

SECTION B: THE NERD HUSBAND

The nerd possesses a charm all his own. Maybe it's his boring predictability, or his unique style of dressing, or just the cute way he snorts when he laughs — but whatever, he is endearing to a lot of women. Many believe nerds make good solid husbands, so here's a list of attributes to look for as a way to I.D. them:

1.   Government-issue black plastic eyeglass frames with tape on the nose bridge

2.   Pocket protectors smeared with blue ball-point ink stains

3.   String tie with sliding silver and turquoise stone holder

4.   Crew Cut loaded with enough wax pomade to spear kabobs

5.   Toothy grin showing class 8 overbite and a lot of gums

6.   White polyester short-sleeve shirt worn with black chino pants and white socks

7.   Pants waist begins up around his chest

8.   Always wears "high water" pants (i.e., cuffs do not reach the ankles)

9.   Carries 500 keys, slide rule, and calculator on brass ring attached to belt loop

10. Wears huge, K Mart label boxer shorts that come down to his knees

11. Death-white skin that has never been exposed to the sun

12. Abundance of facial moles (one for every year of graduate school)

FISCAL TRAITS OF THE NERD

The nerd hubbie is a real planning man. He researches everything and never leaves anything to chance. Each vacation will be pre-planned two years in advance, and he'll study enough books on the subject to write a post-doctoral thesis. You'll be able to stay in student hostels, gather your own food, and ride on off-brand tour buses emitting enough toxic fumes to wipe out entire villages during the entire trip. The approximate cost of touring Europe for a month will be $29.95 excluding tips — which never run above 4.75% anyhow.

He is also not a risk taker in anything he does. Here's a list of the **"Top 10" Behavioral Traits That All Nerds Have In Common**:

10. Never, under any circumstances, removes the tags from mattresses or pillows

9. Always drives 34 miles per hour in a 35 m.p.h. posted zone

8. Gets "high" on doing his taxes

7. Always signals love-making partners he is ready to climax by snorting 10 seconds in advance

6. Never runs while carrying a loaded fountain pen

5. Gets turned on watching "Jeopardy"

4. Considers Alex Trebek the sexiest man alive

3. Is afraid of developing a chemical dependency on Tylenol

2. Considers Chinese takeout to be gourmet dining

And The #1 Nerd Behavioral Trait...

Mails back all of Ed McMahon's Publishers Clearing House Sweepstakes in time to qualify for the Early Bird category

The Nerd sees life from a completely different perspective than the Yuppie. While the Yup spends all his time looking down at the masses, the Nerd looks up at everyone — because his thick bifocal eyeglass frames obscure the lower half of his vision. Working to portray the correct image, the Yup makes sure he is always dressed in his three-piece suit for work, while the Nerd makes sure he always wears his three-piece pajamas to bed. And while the Yup spends his whole life in pursuit of social class, the nerd spends his whole life sitting *in a class*. This gives the Nerd some distinct and unique advantages over the Yuppie husband, including extreme nearsightedness, and the ability to solve problems involving higher math.

In the final analysis, the Nerd will never fit in the social world of the Yup. He'd be like a fish out of water — but all-in-all, some women feel he's not a bad catch.

QUIZ VIII

1. The upscale Yuppie discreetly lets the help know they're services are no longer required by:
   a. running them down with his Beemer
   b. moving their bed and dresser out of the closet
   c. having the kids fire them, for practice
   d. a midnight phone call to the Immigration Department

   * *either a or c is officially sanctioned by the Yuppie Protocol manual*

2. Any self-respecting Yuppie Puppy would never stoop to:
   a. mounting a leg that's not wearing Madras
   b. chewing up a slipper that wasn't imported from Italy
   c. urinating on furniture (unless it is naugahyde)
   d. being paper trained on anything other than the Wall Street Journal

   * *all of the above — and the same goes for their owners*

3. What words will you never find printed on a Yuppie wedding invitation?
   a. "Catholic Church"
   b. "reception at the VFW Hall"
   c. a name ending in a vowel
   d. "bring a covered dish"

   * *all of the above, plus "B.Y.O.B."*

4. Which group is the MOST acceptable for the Yuppie debutante to be presented by?
   a. the Yugoslavian Women's Art Society
   b. El Al Airlines
   c. the United Teamsters Local 101
   d. the Andrew Dice Clay Fan Club of America

   * d — *at no extra cost, Andrew will provide a poetry reading*

5. Which one of the following groups would a Yuppie wife *dare not* belong to:
   a. the Junior League
   b. the DAR
   c. the YPO wives club
   d. the KKK

   * d — *however, an exception will be made if the sheets are designer label*

6. The nerd husband will save his family money by never buying which of the following items:
   a. hair mousse
   b. deodorant
   c. long-sleeve shirts
   d. Compound W

   * a, b, c, d plus anything "in style"

7. The nerd husband protects his clothes from unsightly stains by wearing a:
   a. pocket protector
   b. shirt sleeve protector
   c. armpit protector
   d. crotch protector

   * a — *also <u>d</u> on formal occasions*

CHAPTER 9

OPPOSITES DETRACT:

The Cheating Husband
vs.
The Husband From Heaven

SECTION A:
THE CHEATING HUSBAND

ONCE (Or Twice) IS NOT ENOUGH

The chronic cheating husband is a man who's always been out to grab all the gusto he can get — and a lot of other things, too. In high school, he went steady with two girls at the same time — dating, bedding, and lying to them both on alternate nights as long as he could get away with it. This guy has been such a master at covering up and covering his tracks, he could have been a ghost writer for G. Gordon Liddy. Never satisfied with what he has, the cheater is constantly on the lookout for something better. While walking down the aisle at his own wedding, he's making eyes at the bridesmaids. And when his bride throws her bouquet and her best friend catches it, he's already making plans to de-flower her.

HE'S JUST A GUY WHO CAN'T SAY NO

The cheating husband is a guy who basically never learned to just say "no." He is totally incapable of grasping the simple concept that when you're married, you should only be sleeping with your wife. Case in point: when asked if he knows the difference between fornication and adultery, he'll give this astute reply:

"Well, I've tried both, and I certainly can't tell any difference between them."

CUTTING TO THE CHASE

Psychology books tell us that it's the thrill of the pursuit that these personality types crave rather than the actual sex act itself. This pathetic attempt to explain the situation ranks up there in credibility along with such classics as "The check is in the mail" and "I promise I'll wear a condom." It's obvious to us women that these psychology books must have been written by male psychiatrists who wear silk ascots and have been sued for divorce on grounds of adultery countless times themselves. Any woman who breathes knows that there's no chance any living male on the planet would spend all his time, money, and energy sneaking around to wine and dine a woman, then stop short without having his "just desserts," too.

The truth is that there are a lot of men who absolutely cannot resist a female body in any way, shape or form — literally. But these kinds of husbands rarely accomplish what they set out to do. They always leave such humongous clues in their wake that it leaves us wondering if they really want to get caught. Here are a few of the cheating husband's many "subtle" clues which should alert you that something is up (and it's probably a certain part of his anatomy):

a. When he develops a serious Binaca dependency
b. When the big slob begins using deodorant
c. When he starts using so much cologne that his motto becomes: "I reek, therefore I am"
d. When he insists you start Cloroxing all his gray jockey shorts

Here is some evidence you need to look for when you suspect he is having a fling, raging affair, or a one-night stand:

1. When you find his American Express card loaded with motel bills which have been charged by the half-hour. Also, any restaurant receipts totaling more than $11.99 for dinner-for-two at any establishment other than the Sizzler — which is the only place where he regularly takes you to dine.

2. When he confesses to being a cross-dresser after you find a bra and panties in his glove compartment.

3. When he begins taking three-hour lunches and returns with his jockey shorts on backwards.

4. When you have had your tubes tied for five years and he insists on having a vasectomy "just to be *safe.*"

5. When he starts ordering prophylactics designed with so many feathers, scales, and projections they look more like birds than condoms.

6. When he comes home from a five hour "poker game" reeking of Giorgio instead of cigars.

7. When he replaces all those old baggy boxer shorts with new spandex bikini briefs — with the cup so fully padded, it can compete with your bras.

8. When you haven't had sex for months yet he begins to develop those telltale bed sores on his elbows and knees.

9. When he starts drawing diagrams detailing the exact location of the G-Spot.

10. When you catch him in a phone conversation in which he's whispering "Baby, baby — I need to feel your hot hands on me" and he swears he was talking to his mother.

THE M.O. OF THE P.I.

When your man becomes suspect, it's time to get smart and roll into action by hiring yourself the best P.I. in town to blow him out of the water. But don't expect any glamorous guy who looks like Magnum, p.i. These men all seem to bear an uncanny resemblance to Homer Simpson.

Your first meeting will be under a shroud of secrecy. You'll be asked to drive to a local mall parking lot and wait in your car while wearing a Richard Nixon Halloween mask. Then the P.I. will cautiously approach your car, wearing the obligatory trenchcoat and mirrored sunglasses. He will try to appear as inconspicuous as possible, but his cover will be blown within three seconds by a crowd of female ex-clients in the parking lot who instantly recognize him from past business dealings. They will conspicuously point at him saying:

"Why, there's Dick Sleezeball, the town P.I.! Wanna bet that masked woman in the Honda over there is having her cheating husband tailed!"

Meanwhile, Sleezeball will slip into the back seat and tell you not to turn around and look at him while you're talking. This is Standard Operating Procedure to avoid arousing suspicion — and arousing him, too, because that Richard Nixon mask in the front seat really turns him on. What he doesn't understand is that it's hard not to pique the curiosity of passersby when they see a person in a

Richard Nixon mask in the front seat and one in a Jason mask in the back seat on a Saturday morning in a Civic. But, being the consummate professional, he'll ask you to produce the following info on the suspect husband:

1. A recent shot of him — preferably *au naturél*, so he can get a positive ID on the offending parts in case your husband's face is covered by a sheet during the photo opportunity.

2. A pair of jockey shorts bearing recent lipstick prints for a positive ID check on the suspect paramour.

3. The make of his car and designer sheets covering the back seat.

4. Any credit card receipts for suspicious purchases like handcuffs, cases of Wesson oil, or an elastic gut cincher with velcro closings.

5. Any change in his normal behavioral patterns like a sudden enrollment in night school to take classes in sewing, English for displaced persons, or home maintenance.

6. A new-found interest in his appearance. Like ditching the old "wet-head" look for a trendy hairstyle utilizing so much mousse, he's sprouting antlers.

7. A receipt for the mail order item identified as the "Belly Burner"; the home exerciser which is supposed to take inches off your gut in just two short weeks. (This is such a dead giveaway in proving an affair is raging, that divorce courts routinely base their settlements on the possession of one of these gizmos.)

8. A phone tap producing a high-quality recording of any of the following*
   — grunts
   — moans
   — heavy breathing
   — or any evidence of moisture
     * spoken words are allegedly not admissible evidence in the courtroom.
9. The reciprocating Fax number of the party he sent the photostatic copy of his private parts to. (The confirmation sheet stating the quality of the transmission as being "inadequate" will help, too.)
10. Any evidence of phone cord meltdown from late night steamy phone conversations.

For your $100 bucks an hour plus expenses, in all probability you'll get a report back within a week containing the following "evidence":

1. A blurred photograph of his car showing two smudged footprints on the side rear window.
2. A videotape of your husband grabbing the mike at the Ramada Inn's Lizard Lounge, crooning "Strangers In The Night" to his young bimbo, who is clad in black leather and revealing more cleavage than Elvira.
3. A shocking photo of the two of them in a hotel room showing your husband clad in your bra and panties, and tied to the headboard with leather thongs. The paramour is front and center, wearing her Gestapo nightie and apparently flogging him with her leather pantyhose. This evidence will add a new facet to your case, because you are now able to fault him not only

on the grounds of adultery, but also on the hilarious attempted execution of lewd sex acts.

4. A photo taken in a porno movie house with a special infrared lens which shows him wearing a trenchcoat and a silly grin. A photo enlargement reveals the existence of a trick popcorn box on his lap in which his lover's arm has disappeared up to her elbow.

5. A videotape of the two of them exiting a cramped airplane restroom, with him frantically trying to stuff her panty hose into his jacket pocket. She proceeds back to her seat with a telltale water ring from the sink on the back of her dress.

After you've got your evidence, you're off to court. This may be a time-consuming process, but there are lots of productive and fun things you can do to pass the time while you're waiting for your divorce to happen. The first thing many women do, if their divorce lawyer looks like Arnie Becker and not Marvin Mitchelson, is to have yourself a hot fling of your own.

Then, when you meet Mr. Right and are contemplating another marriage, give him this acid test. After professing his dying love and promising to be faithful forever, take him to the hottest singles bar in town. If he can get through the evening without so much as glancing at any of those barracuda babes, he's either:

a. impotent
b. going to be faithful

In either case, you won't lose — he'll never cheat on you. So marry him.

SECTION B: THE HEAVENLY HUSBAND

HE'S JUST TOO GOOD TO BE TRUE: THE HUSBAND FROM HEAVEN

Every woman's dream is to end up with the perfect man: a.k.a. the Husband from Heaven. He's a loving family man who honors the old-fashioned values of fidelity, courtesy, and honesty between husband and wife. This is a man who works hard at maintaining harmony in your relationship by always putting your needs before his own. The heavenly hubbie places you on a pedestal; he adores you.

He's also neat and well-groomed, hangs up his own clothes, doesn't drink, smoke, or leave his dirty T-shirts and socks turned inside-out for you to launder. What a guy!!

The Husband from Heaven is as close to perfection as you can get. Here are some of his most admirable traits:

1. Balances the checkbook to the penny and pays all the bills on time
2. Never forgets to send roses on your birthday and anniversary
3. Supports you emotionally
4. Never picks fights or raises his voice during discussions
5. Never gives you a Weed-Whacker for your birthday
6. Takes the kids out on Saturdays so you can have a day off
7. Allows you to have cleaning help twice a week so you can play tennis or go shopping for clothes
8. Calls twice a day to say he loves you

9.* Lets you slap him around, if necessary, during your PMS fits

10.* Gives you an unlimited clothing allowance

*(9. and 10. being the most desirable of all traits)

And in the area of making love, he's truly a dream:

1. Brushes his teeth and uses mouthwash BEFORE you make love
2. Takes great direction during foreplay
3. Volunteers for a vasectomy during the delivery of your second child
4. Satisfies you first, and never complains when you roll over and fall asleep immediately afterwards
5. Unties you promptly after a bondage session
6. Takes FLATTERING pictures of you in the nude
7. Wouldn't THINK of approaching you at your time of the month
8. Promptly replaces dead batteries in all marital aids
9. Never forgets to put the cap back on the KY jelly
10. Doesn't mind when you talk all the way through sex — even if it's long distance

Is this guy from heaven or what? He's thoughtful, considerate, compliant, ...submissive, subservient, and come to think of it — a downright wimp. Geez Louise! You'll never be able to engage in a good old-fashioned knock-down, drag-out rip-roaring fight, or a night of wild-abandon sex, or share a good dirty joke with this man! He's so consumed with doing everything right that life has become totally predictable. And you're bored to death.

But of course gals, in reality, you'll never have to cope with these kinds of problems. Why? Because the Husband from Heaven simply does not exist.

QUIZ IX

1. Women who marry cheating husbands have:
   a. a need to be punished
   b. short term memory loss
   c. a lot of free *nights*
   d. something on the side, themselves

   * d — *if they're smart*

2. The cheating husband's theme song is:
   a. "Do It To Me One More Time" by Toni Tenielle
   b. "Me So Horny" by 2 Live Crew
   c. "Afternoon Delight" by Starlight Vocal Band
   d. "Nobody Does It Better" by Carly Simon

   * d — *makes his paramour sing it to him while making love*

3. The cheating husband's wife's favorite movie is:
   a. "I'm Gonna Git You Sucka"
   b. "No Way Out"
   c. "sex, lies, and videotape"
   d. "Fatal Attraction"

   * c — *home version, which can be used in court*

4. The best way to catch the cheating husband is with:
   a. the help of a discreet P.I.
   b. careful documentation of his activities
   c. detailed record of phone calls and expenses
   d. his pants down

   * d — *eliminates the need for a, b, or c*

5. The husband from heaven will give you unlimited:
   a. credit
   b. cash
   c. cleaning help
   d. sex

   * *a,b,c,d — and you can never have too much of any of it*

EPILOGUE

So there you have it, gals — the whole spectrum of husbands available out there. And considering what's available at this point, your future must be looking bleaker by the minute. It's enough to make you want to gulp down a bunch of Valium and Prozac with your three martini lunch now, isn't it? One thing is for sure — you're not exactly in the mood to go out and do the rhumba with Tito Fuentes.

But look at the up-side here. You have been enlightened from this discourse — and forewarned is forearmed. There are some redeeming qualities in every man. The trick is to find them. Let's face facts. We women aren't exactly perfect either. Close — but not exactly perfect. There are times when we slip up — like only ironing 10 shirts instead of 12, or missing a few tiles with our grout brush when we scrub the bathroom floors every day, or forgetting to add yeast to our freshly baked bread. But the one thing we can say with all honesty is that we are always OBJECTIVE about ourselves.

So what are we going to do? How do we find our DREAM man the second time around? We would desire a combination of the best attributes in the book. We will look for a husband who incorporates all of these qualities:
- is young — but experienced
- has money — but doesn't flaunt it
- is sexually athletic — but doesn't overdo it

171

- is a professional — but not a *boss*
- is neat — but without being an anal retentive
- is healthy — but likes cheeseburgers
- is handy around the house — but his collection of tools fits neatly inside a *small* case
- doesn't cheat on you — and doesn't mind if you *playfully flirt* with other men

Just keep telling yourself that there is a man out there who has it all, and YOU can have him — the perfect man. And then go to bed and find him waiting for you — in your dreams!

GLOSSARY OF HUSBANDS FROM HELL

THE SLOB HUSBAND — a man who wouldn't know what a laundry basket was if it bit him on the butt. Unlike intelligent species in the Animal Kingdom, he usually ends up fouling his nest — especially in the bathroom, where he's known for laying "rotten eggs."

THE PERFECTIONIST (ANAL RETENTIVE) HUSBAND — a man whose compulsive behavior is so irritating, he could drive Mother Teresa to commit a violent act. The opposite of the slob when it comes to cleanliness, he'll spend hours in the bathroom disinfecting the sink, the toilet, and his bottom.

THE BLUE COLLAR HUSBAND — this burly guy is known for his rugged approach to life. He likes his women like his pickup truck — fully charged, easy to handle, and well lubricated.

THE PROFESSIONAL HUSBAND — the most sought-after type of all, they sit in big offices and make big bucks. But be cautioned about those mega-buck salaries, because besides supporting you they can also comfortably support two or three future families. So don't be the wife who got the distinction of sharing his past — and like it, you became history.

THE YOUNGER HUSBAND — these marriages are a study in role reversal where you get to become his "teacher" in all areas, except in the bedroom where this kid will end up giving *you* the education. Then you'll become the willing pupil, spending hours every night on your "homework."

THE OLDER HUSBAND — this is a guy who is pleasing to the senses. Be sure to choose one who has aged like the bouquet of a fine wine and reeks of old money too.

THE HYPOCHONDRIAC HUSBAND — although all his pain is in his head, the wife of the hypochondriac feels it at the opposite end of her anatomy.

THE HELPLESS HUSBAND — more helpless than a two-year-old, this man must never be left alone in the house. He could die of starvation because he can't operate a can opener, will electrocute himself blow-drying his hair in the shower, or suffocate while trying to lick the crumbs out of a plastic Doritos bag.

THE DO-IT-YOURSELF HUSBAND — a guy who spends an inordinate amount of time in his tool shed sharpening his adz and greasing his nuts. Poised with a fully-loaded tool belt slung around his hips, he would certainly merit the description of being "well hung." But of course, not in the vernacular WE care about!

THE HEALTH NUT HUSBAND — spends hours "pumping up" his body to a point where it begins to look like one of those giant figures floating over New York in the Macy's Thanksgiving Day Parade. He could qualify as an entry, because his stomach produces enough gas from eating organic beans to keep himself aloft.

THE COUCH POTATO HUSBAND — has about as much "get-up and go" as a snail on Valium. There's not much that can get this man to move off the couch except for maybe a full bedpan — or the discovery that he left the remote control on top of the TV.

THE PARTY ANIMAL HUSBAND — a guy who truly believes that after having a few drinks, he'll be perfectly sober once he gets behind the wheel of his car. And when he's pulled over by a cop, does not fare well when asked to show his identification — and he drops his pants.

THE SEXUAL ATHLETE HUSBAND — every woman's favorite kind of guy. Is able to make love under ANY kind of circumstance — including your absence.

THE SEXUALLY UNATHLETIC HUSBAND — is a man who thinks that "getting it up" means being excited about an airshow.

THE YUPPIE HUSBAND — always striving to portray that upper class image, inside and out, he will go to such lengths as purchasing pin-striped condoms to match his Burberry shirts.

THE NERD HUSBAND — a man who's never without his slide rule. He's a very handy guy to have around. He can instantaneously convert U.S. measures and weights to Metric, figure out exactly how many square feet of carpeting you'll need in your home, and calculate within six seconds your exact time of ovulation.

THE CHEATING HUSBAND — lives by the credo "Two in the bush are worth one in the hand." His hobbies include nude photography, making X-rated home videos, and frequent court appearances.

THE HUSBAND FROM HEAVEN — aptly called the "man of your dreams" — this is the only place where he truly exists.

ABOUT THE AUTHOR

Photo by Philip Bermingham

Jan King is the author of the best selling book *Hormones From Hell.* Her inspiration for that book came from an 18 year menopause and surviving several mid-life crises. Her background information for "Husbands" was derived from having two marriages she admits to, and undoubtedly countless more to which she doesn't. Any similarities which her girlfriends' husbands find to themselves in any of the chapters was probably purely intentional.

She lives in McLean, Virginia, with her two teenage sons whom she tries to pass off as her brothers on good days when she's not retaining fluid.

TITLES BY CCC PUBLICATIONS

—NEW BOOKS—

HUSBANDS FROM HELL

THE Unofficial WOMEN'S DIVORCE GUIDE

FOR **MEN** ONLY (How To Survive Marriage)

HORMONES FROM HELL (The Ultimate *Women's* Humor Book)

GIFTING RIGHT (How To Give A Great Gift Every Time! For Any Occasion! And On Any Budget!)

THE SUPERIOR PERSON'S GUIDE TO EVERYDAY IRRITATIONS

HOW TO TALK YOUR WAY OUT OF A TRAFFIC TICKET

YOUR GUIDE TO CORPORATE SURVIVAL

WHAT DO WE DO NOW?? (The Complete Guide For All New Parents Or Parents-To-Be)

—SUMMER 1991 RELEASES—

HOW TO REALLY PARTY!!!

THE GUILT BAG [Accessory Item]

THE ABSOLUTE LAST CHANCE DIET BOOK

—BEST SELLERS—

NO HANG-UPS (Funny Answering Machine Messages)

NO HANG-UPS II

NO HANG-UPS III

GETTING EVEN WITH THE ANSWERING MACHINE

HOW TO GET EVEN WITH YOUR EXes

HOW TO SUCCEED IN SINGLES BARS

TOTALLY OUTRAGEOUS BUMPER-SNICKERS

THE "MAGIC BOOKMARK" BOOK COVER [Accessory Item]

—CASSETTES—

NO HANG-UPS TAPES (Funny, Pre-recorded Answering Machine Messages With Hilarious *Sound Effects*) — In Male or Female Voices

Vol. I: GENERAL MESSAGES

Vol. II: BUSINESS MESSAGES

Vol. III: 'R' RATED

Vol. IV: SOUND EFFECTS ONLY

Vol. V: CELEBRI-TEASE (Celebrity Impersonations)

Coming Soon:

Vol. VI: MESSAGES FOR SPORTS FANS